THE CATHOLIC UNIVERSITY OF AMERICA
CANON LAW STUDIES
No. 120

PRINCIPLES OF EPISCOPAL JURISDICTION

A DISSERTATION IN
PUBLIC ECCLESIASTICAL LAW

Submitted to the Faculty of Canon Law of the Catholic University of America in Partial Fulfillment of the Requirements for the Degree of

DOCTOR OF CANON LAW

BY

GERALD ALOYSIUS RYAN, A.B., J.C.L.
Priest of the Archdiocese of Philadelphia

THE CATHOLIC UNIVERSITY OF AMERICA PRESS
WASHINGTON, D. C.
1939

NIHIL OBSTAT:
EDUARDUS G. ROELKER, S.T.D., J.C.D.,
Censor Deputatus.
Washingtonii, die 2 Junii, 1939.

IMPRIMATUR:
✠ D. CARD. DOUGHERTY,
Archiepiscopus Philadelphiensis.
Philadelphia, die 6 Junii, 1939.

PRINTED IN THE UNITED STATES OF AMERICA
BY THE WATKINS PRINTING CO., BALTIMORE

IN
HONOREM
SPIRITUS SANCTI
QUI
POSUIT
EPISCOPOS
REGERE
ECCLESIAM
DEI

CONTENTS

FOREWORD

The scope of this discussion is exactly indicated in the terms of its title, which at first sight may seem to imply much more than is intended. It is limited, first of all, to *principles,* the source and standard rather than the stream and structure of power; secondly, to principles of *jurisdiction,* the social authority (*regimen*) rather than the sacramental power (*ministerium*) of the Church; thirdly, to principles of *episcopal* jurisdiction, which herein connotes only the authority of the Residential Bishop.

The principles of the Church's power as found decreed in Spripture and apostolic tradition, have been preserved and developed throughout History, explained in Theology, and crystallized in Law. The juridical aspect of the Episcopate, then, as a canonical institute expounded in Public Law, that branch of legal science which treats of principles and to which this treatment is confined, is the immediate consequence of theological tenets derived in turn from divine revelation and historical record. The canonist, however, will properly restrict himself to his own field when, in realizing that the results of postulate sciences are the roots of his own, he accepts them as already proven suppositions, and attends to their specifically canonical implications.

The subject naturally divides itself into two general sections, the first dealing with the status, the second with the function of the episcopate; that is, treating respectively, and in philosophic progression, of the being and the action, a division to which the Code of Canon Law, in its summary but sufficient statement of the propositions involved, conveniently lends itself in Canons 329 and 335. Moreover, while these statements in themselves are primarily of doctrinal import, as presented in the Code(which, though intentionally disciplinary, must necessarily at times be doctrinal) they do not precisely contain or propose a doctrine as such, but a doctrine which is necessarily generative of a discipline so immediately consequential as to be almost concomitant to it. The teaching, therefore, is not new but is, as it were, clothed in a new dress intentionally expressive of its juridical significance; and this study will limit itself to an exposition of the subject (the exegetical and apologetic foundations of which are presupposed) as found in the Canons which set forth anew the ancient principles of diocesan government.

The author takes occasion here sincerely to thank His Eminence Dennis Cardinal Dougherty, Archbishop of Philadelphia, for the opportunity of advanced study, and all who in any way contributed to the preparation of this work for their interest and aid.

INTRODUCTION

INTRODUCTION

Article 1

Previous Commentary on the Episcopate

The episcopate may be viewed from many distinct angles. There is possible, first of all, the separate consideration of episcopal Orders and of episcopal jurisdiction. Each of these has a theological import which may be treated either apologetically or positively, historically or according to its present status. The latter has also a juridical import which may be viewed from the standpoint of either private or public law. This last aspect is the present concern, and it is a distinct one. For while the several possible views of the episcopate are not and cannot possibly be altogether mutually exclusive, but are and must be interrelated rather than isolated, there is in each sufficient worth to lend it an individuality which warrants particular consideration.

The science of public ecclesiastical law is a comparatively new one. Until the twelfth century all ecclesiastical law was regarded scientifically as a part of theology, which itself was not as now divided adequately into dogmatic and moral as separate treatises. From then until the eighteenth century no distinction was made between public and private law. The principles with which public law deals are as old as the Church. The earliest patristic writings attest both to their general acceptance and to the occasional need for defending them. The apologetic aspect was then as now recognized as the province of theology. Apologetics, however, develops as the attack which it repels occasions. Thus, in the post-Reformation world there arose the first real need for the apologetic presentation of the Church's institution, constitution and organization, because the Reformers had seriously attacked the legitimacy of the visible social organism. Later, as a result of the nationalistic influences of the reformation and the ultimate extolling of the state over the Church as the final determinant of right and wrong, the need arose for the defense of the Church against the encroachments of the state. With the fundamental theses on the Church written by the apologetes, the canonists began to assert the juridical implications of the theological tenets, and to define the relative positions in the world of Church and state. This original treatment of the Church as a society from the canonical standpoint was not concerned so much with the internal constitution as with the external relation of the Church to the civil society. The basis of the principles which they formulated was, indeed, the internal constitution of the ecclesiastical society, and though it would logically precede, the exposition of the Church's internal organization chronologically followed the explanation of the Church's external relations.

The various juridical implications of the theological tenets concerning the Church as a society have for the most part been thus far adequately and ably defended and defined. There are, however, parts which for some reason or other have been consistently neglected, ignored, or at most implied in the general treatises which have appeared in the field of public internal law within the last century. Among them is the episcopate and its particular implications. One of the reasons for this may be the fact that since the *Summa Theologica* of St. Thomas Aquinas most, if not all, theologians have incorporated into their works the questions proposed and discussed by the Angelic Doctor, and the *Summa* as written by St. Thomas contains no comprehensive or systematic treatment of the episcopate as an organic part of the divinely instituted ecclesiastical society. Consequently, when taking the theological tenets on which to build their juridical structure, the canonists were at first able to find little on which to expatiate, and hesitated to excogitate regarding the episcopate from this particular standpoint.

Moreover, there was no recognized immediate practical need for such a treatise. The science of public law originated as an indirect result of the Reformation at a time when the Church in general was attacked as a society coordinate to the state rather than as any particular species of social organization or in any specific detail thereof. It developed for the most part within the last century at a time when the episcopate was in pacific possession of its traditional and vigorously defended rights, howsoever vaguely they were defined. The immediate need for such a treatment as the following purports to be was, therefore, not existent either during the time of birth or of the growth of public law as a science. Such an exposition of principles, however, though rather speculative in itself, will always be as practical as the foundation of a house. The author of the Church, Christ, has planned, the apostles have laid the foundations, and the Church itself must continue to build thereon, but only in accordance with the plan, within the limits of the original foundations, and according to the design decreed by the Architect.

There are, to be sure, numerous works published on the subject of the episcopate. For the most part, however, they are from the viewpoint of private canon law, and except by way of passing, as in the works of the theologians also, they do not inquire into or set forth the particular basic characteristics of the episcopate in any frame whereby their social and organic import or implications are adequately proportioned. In all the manuals thus far published on the subject of public law, the episcopate holds a rather small space if any. It is generally deemed enough to explain and expound the power of the Church in general and of the Roman Pontiff in particular, and to allow that of the bishop to be derived, since it is implicitly contained in the latter. The definition of the Roman Primacy in the last century helps to determine definitely the power of the bishop, variously attacked and extolled beyond its capacity by the Febronians, Gallicans and others.

At first, as with all ecclesiastical doctrine, the exposition of episcopal power was but vaguely determined, and only on occasion of attack or abuse was any particular point on it brought out in clear lines. Thus, the scriptural evidence, the patristic testimony, etc., all attest to the fact of episcopal authority but lend little to the explicit statement of the juridic theory. The Code of Canon Law, however, contains several express propositions from which the whole doctrine of episcopal jurisdiction can be conveniently derived.

Article 2

Social Character of the Church

The point of departure of a treatise on Episcopal Jurisdiction is that the Catholic Church, the uniquely authentic and legitimate manifestation of Christianity, is a society juridically perfect in its nature and hierarchic in its divinely distributed personal organization. The general notion of the Church as such is fundamental to any particular study in Public Ecclesiastical Law.

I. Juridical Perfection

Generically, any society is a union of men for the attainment of a common end by common means. This definition indicates the only requisite and sufficient elements of the *integrally* perfect society. It is a moral entity because its formal cause is the moral union of its material members. Christianity, therefore, the legacy which Christ left to the world for the continuance and the completion of His work,[1] was eminently adaptable as a social medium thereto; for while Christ taught a particular doctrine in which all men must believe,[2] it is also, and necessarily, a practical doctrine, belief in which not only precedes but postulates a common behaviour.[3] Moreover, since Christ came to redeem man on the condition that man would cooperate with the spiritual help given him individually by grace, but through the social agency of the Church, Christianity must ever be accepted as a visibly social medium of salvation.[4]

Specifically, however, "societies are distinguished by the purpose they pursue." [5] The end is at once the first cause of the society's existence and the ultimate specific determinant of its nature and juridical status, the sphere and the strength of its

[1] John 15:15; 16:27.

[2] Mark 16:16; John 6:47.

[3] Matt. 7:16, 24; Gal. 3:12; James 3:17.

[4] Conc. Vat., Sess. IV, *Constitutio dogmatica de Ecclesia Christi,* Proemium—ASS, VI (1870), 40.

[5] Augustine, *A Commentary on the New Code of Canon Law* (4. ed., St. Louis: B. Herder, 8 vols., 1921-1925), I, 191.

activity.[6] The more complete and inclusive its aim, the more necessary is the society's existence, and the more requisite its existence, the more adequate and exclusive are its powers, that is, the greater is its *juridical* perfection. Although man as a social being has a double destiny, a temporal and an eternal happiness, there is, in the design of Providence, no one society ordained to satisfy both the natural and the supernatural demands of human nature. The provinces are distinct, though coordinate, and the powers are divided, yet complementary.[7] The actually existent juridically perfect society, then, is that which tends to the total perfection of its own order, and which, as a consequence of its relatively perfect and necessary end, has a native right to all the means necessary thereto, the power to fulfill its purpose.[8] There are but two species of it: the State in each of its manifold national and territorial divisions, and the One Universal Church.[9]

The purpose of the Church is the sanctification and the consequent salvation of souls. This is a supernatural aim and requires a proportionately spiritual agency which, in turn, is resident in a physical social agent. Grace is the treasure with which man must traffic, and good works are the key thereto. As the dispensor of grace the Church exercises her Sacramental ministry. As the director of good works, that is, of faith and of a life according to the faith, she exercises her social mission. For the former office she is endowed by Christ with the power of Orders, and for the latter with the power of Jurisdiction.[10] Since the scope of this discussion embraces professedly only the latter, merely occasional reference will be made to the former more theological question.

[6] Ottaviani, *Institutiones Iuris Publici Ecclesiastici* (2 ed., 2 vols., Typis Polyglottis Vaticanis, 1935), I, n. 21.

[7] Leo XIII, ep. encycl. "*Immortale Dei*", 1 nov. 1885, nn. 24-27—*Fontes*, n. 592.

[8] Ottaviani, *Institutiones Iuris Publici Ecclesiastici*, I, n. 33.

[9] Leo XIII, ep. encycl. "*Immortale Dei*", n. 18—*Fontes*, n. 592.

[10] Piux X, litt. encycl. "*Pascendi*", 8 sept. 1907—*Fontes*, n. 680; St. Thomas Aquinas, *Summa Theologica*, 2a 2ae, q. 39 a. 3: Cappello, *Summa Iuris Publici Ecclesiastici* (2, ed., Romae: Apud Aedes Universitatis Gregorianae, 1929), p. 183.

II. Ecclesiastical Jurisdiction

In its present canonical use the term *jurisdiction,* which etymologically (*"ius dicere"*) conveys at the most a vague, and at the least an ambiguous notion of any specific power, has a much more extensive significance than its original and (according to the most general acceptance) its ordinary meaning in Roman Law. In Roman Law usage jurisdiction implied merely the official act of declaring subjective rights and duties relative to the law. It was, therefore, restricted to the *judicial* authority in the modern sense, or the power to take cognizance of causes and to decide them according to law or equity; [11] although there is evidence of a late tendency toward a less restrictive employment of the word to designate a somewhat general administrative power.[12] It was rather in this sense that the Church adopted the term, and since the time of Gregory the Great (590-604), although in canonical terminology from the seventh to the twelfth century the word itself is not of frequent occurrence,[13] it has when employed by canonists consistently denoted the whole power of government inherent in the juridically perfect society as such, both civil and ecclesiastical.[14]

Nominally, then, *ecclesiastical* jurisdiction comprises the entire social power (*regimen*) of the Church.[15] Even this somewhat generic concept excludes any direct notion of the power of Orders (*ministerium*). Her Sacramental ministry, which regards prim-

[11] "La giurisdizione nel diritto romano era esclusivamente limitata alla decisione delle controversie giuridiche civili."—I. Glück, *Commentario alle Pandette* (2 vols., Milano, 1888), II, 5.

[12] Cf. Van DeKerekhove, "De Notione Iurisdictionis in Iure Romano," *Jus Pontificium,* XVI (1936), 49-65.

[13] For instances of expressions used synonymously, especially in councils of the period (e. g., *"subjectum habere," "canonice commendatum habere,"* etc.) cf. Van DeKerekhove, *loc. cit.*

[14] "Jurisdictio est potestas publica circa aliorum regimen seu gubernationem."—Reiffenstuel, *Ius Canonicum Universum* (4 vols., Romae, 1843-1844), lib. I, tit. I, n. 29.

[15] "Jurisdictio est potestas regendi fideles in ordine ad salutem aeternam." —Prümmer, Dominicus, *Manuale Iuris Canonici,* (4. ed., Friburgi: Herder, 1927), p. 119.

arily the individual good, is not essentially a part of the Church's social power; it can only be considered social in the sense that it is a social possession and that its use, which by Christ's disposition is a social duty, must like any social means be regulated by the social authority.[16]

The actual power implied by this concept, on the other hand, embraces not only the disciplinary authority (*imperium*) common to all juridically perfect societies, but also a doctrinal prerogative *(magisterium)* proper exclusively to the ecclesiastical body, in virtue of which the Church authoritatively controls not only the behaviour but also the belief of her members. Acceptance of and adherence to Christian truth is the only sufficient motive cause of Christian conduct, and consequently it is a postulate of the Church's social aim; so that a necessary right of the Church *as a society* is the power to teach and to command assent to those doctrines in accordance with and concerning which she formulates her disciplinary rule.[17]

Moreover, while in other perfect societies the jurisdictional power extends to the individual member of the society only in his relation to the society itself, the peculiar nature of the Church's purpose necessitates its extension also to the individual's moral relation to God. That is to say, it embraces both the external and the internal forum,[18] the latter because the purpose of the Church is the sanctification of *individuals* directly,[19] a condition which finally depends on the individual's relation to God, and from which the common good derives.[20] However, although the reverse is not true, a jurisdictional act of the external forum is effective also

[16] Cf. canon 210.

[17] Billot, *Tractatus De Ecclesia Christi* (4. ed., 2 vols., Romae: Apud Aedes Universitatis Gregorianae, 1921), I, 343.

[18] Canon 196; "Ad forum externum pertinent actiones quibus fideles in facie Ecclesiae iusti aut rei fiunt, ad internum actiones qua iusti aut rei sunt coram Deo."—Vermeersh-Creusen, *Epitome Iuris Canonici* (6. ed., 3 vols., Mechliniae: Dessain, 1937), I, n. 313.

[19] Solieri, *Institutiones Iuris Ecclesiastici* (2. ed., Romae: Pustet, 1921), p. 179.

[20] Solieri, *op. cit.*, p. 180.

in the internal,[21] so that in dealing directly with the former it is unnecessary to treat of the latter expressly. These remarks suffice to explain the nature of that power signified generally and herein by the term ecclesiastical jurisdiction;[22] it remains to examine the personnel to which it is entrusted.

Article 3

Personal Design of the Church

I. Notion of Authority

As a moral and a juridic entity, the perfect society is not and cannot be or remain static. It is by analogy dignified with the title of person. The ultimate basis of such a comparison of the perfect society to the human individual is the fact that the former like the latter possesses by its nature certain essential rights. The practical reason, however, for the conception of the society as a person is that it is necessarily active in the preservation of its rights. Its activity is concerned with the ordination of its means to its end. Furthermore it must both exist and act as a unit if it is to pursue its purpose effectively. The principle of this unity, required both to obtain and to preserve it, is *authority.* As the preservative principle of that unity which formally constitutes the society, authority is the social representative, the embodiment of the moral personality in one or more physical members thereof. As the constitutive principle of that unity which must characterize the social activity, authority is the social ruler,[23] the embodiment of the juridic power in one or more of the social members. While, as has been said, the nature and the extent of this juridic power is determined by the social purpose, the personal organization to which it is intrusted and in which it

[21] Canon 202 § 1.

[22] "Potestas gregem Christi regendi, tum quoad intellectum per doctrinam rectae fidei, quae praecepti ritu credenda proponitur, tum quoad voluntatem per verum proprieque dictum imperium, quo tota mediorum oeconomia fideles diriguntur, ita ut ipsa quoque sacramentorum dispensatio ad eiusmodi potestatis officium pertineat."—Tarquini, *Iuris Ecclesiastici Publici Institutiones* (4. ed., Romae, 1875), p. 82.

[23] Leo XIII, ep. encycl. *"Immortale Dei"*, n. 18,—*Fontes,* n. 592.

actively resides depends on the will and disposition of the society's founder and author.[24]

The official power of the Church, both Sacramental and social, is radically invested in one person, the Pope. He may be considered as an absolute monarch in one sense, and in another sense as a constitutional monarch. He is an absolute monarch in the sense that his power as supreme in spiritual matters cannot be vetoed by any other authority on earth within or without the Church. He is a constitutional monarch in that he is bound by the fundamental laws of the Church as constituted by Christ. In virtue of the constitution of the Church as established by Christ, although the Pope is the supreme, he is not the sole authority.[25] The power of the Church is not isolated in his person, but is also vested in the body of the clergy, those set apart under him by Christ to teach, govern and minister to the faithful.[26] The clergy, moreover, while distinct from the body of the laity, as superiors from their subjects, are hierarchically distinguished among themselves.[27]

II. Ecclesiastical Hierarchy

"In general, we mean by Hierarchy (*lit.* 'sacred government') the ministers or officials of the Church arranged in ranks according to the degree of spiritual power or authority which they possess."[28] It is a constitutional feature of the Church in both its ministry and its government.[29] As such its various fundamental divisions must, potentially at least, coincide originally with the origin of the ecclesiastical society. For the Church was left to

[24] Ottaviani, *Institutiones Iuris Publici Ecclesiastici,* I, nn. 29-30.

[25] "Si Petri eiusque successorum plena ac summa potestas est, ea tamen esse ne putetur sola"—Leo XIII, ep. encycl. *"Satis cognitum"*, 29 ium. 1896, n. 25—*Fontes,* n. 630.

[26] Canon 107; Conc. Trid., Sess. XXIII, *de ordine,* c. 4,—Mansi, *Sacrorum Conciliorum Nova et Amplissima Collectio,* (53 vols., Parisiis, 1901-1927), XXIII, 138.

[27] Canon 108, §2.

[28] Sheehan, *Apologetics and Christian Doctrine* (2. ed., Dublin: Gill and Son, 1929), p. 201.

[29] Canon 108, §3.

be perfected by time. Its constitution as determined by Christ contained the same elements which the course of history has evolved to their present fulness.

In conferring the powers with which He endowed His Church, that of Orders peculiar to her sacramental ministry, and that of jurisdiction, the prerogative of her social mission, Christ ordained only to the *Fulness of the Priesthood,* and He so ordained only those on whom He also bestowed complete command. The same persons were anointed pastors of individual souls as were appointed prefects of the entire flock. Thus, at the start, the natural correlation of the two species of power is more apparent than the difference between them. This will probably always be so, for since the clergy in general form the governing body in the Church,[30] and since one of the most important of the Church's immediate social purposes is its spiritual ministry, it would seem to follow that ordinarily one with jurisdiction will also be one in Orders, and that the higher the one the greater the other.[31]

The more important consideration herein, however, is the fact that, though correlative, the two powers are essentially distinct, and that even if they were not always so apparently distinct as now, they have nevertheless always been separably existent.[32] They differ principally in immediate origin and purpose. The one is directly conferred by ordination, the other by canonical mission. The one is directly intended for the individual, the other for the social benefit.[33] Until almost the twelfth century these elements of distinction and separability were not so evident, since it was customary to confer the canonical mission on the occasion of ordination, a fact which is still attested in the rite of episcopal consecration.[34] Even yet the difference is, unfortunately, all too

[30] Canon 118.

[31] "Deinceps, si ecclesiae divinae instituionis factum attendatur, Christus voluit ut qui primum et secundum iurisdictionis gradum *iure divino* consecuti sint, Ordinis etiam plenitudine ornarentur, imo illum Romae Episcopum designavit."—Solieri, *Institutiones Iuris Ecclesiastici,* p. 55.

[32] Ottaviani, *Institutiones Iuris Publici Ecclesiastici,* I, n. 114.

[33] Cappello, *Summa Iuris Publici Ecclesiastici,* pp. 183-187.

[34] *Pontificale Romanum, De Consecratione Electi in Episcopum.*

frequently regarded as rather more academic than practical, with the result that many issues hinging on it remain today as confused as formerly. For much of the error and confusion in historical criticism and canonical commentary is due either to ignorance of or inadvertence to this fact, as well as to the possibility, advisability, or even necessity of discussing the powers separately.

With this independence and interrelation in mind, a further distinction is necessary regarding the grades in each of the powers. As to both species, the hierarchy of *powers* is essential, but the hierarchy of *persons* is a requisite only in jurisdiction. "The Council of Trent in defining that the Hierarchy of Orders is of divine institution did not mean that the Church has necessarily three distinct classes of ministers, but three distinct degrees of spiritual power,[35] comprised in the Fulness of the Priesthood.

As to jurisdiction, both the hierarchy of powers and that of persons is necessary, nor was this hierarchical division ever merely potential, as in the case of Orders before the apostles had begun to share their power with others, but was actually established as such by Christ personally, and can never be abolished, for in the apostolic college there was a hierarchy both of powers and of persons.

Even antecedently to the positive will of Christ which makes it *de iure* necessary, the jurisdictional hierarchy of *powers* would seem to be at least *de facto expedient*. For while the catholicity of the Church, the world-wide extent of her mission, practically requires at once a distinct universal and a territorial authority, the unity of the Church demands that the one be supreme and the other subordinate. Moreover, because by divine disposition. while the two powers are *generically* one (i. e., *episcopal*), their hierarchical relation results not merely from a difference in local extent or relative finality but more radically from an essential difference in *specific* nature and scope, it would seem likewise fitting that there should be a correlative hierarchy of jurisdictional *persons*, that is, that the two jurisdictional powers should *de facto* be, as indeed they *de iure* are, invested in different persons, the

[35] Sheehan, *Apologetics and Christian Doctrine*, p. 201.

Roman Pontiff and the residental bishops respectively. The juridical relation of the two results from and is specified by the personal monarchic primacy of the former, that plenitude of power to which the authority of the latter is, somewhat aristocratically,[36] associated.

Consequently, just as there must always be bishops in the Church to provide for its spiritual ministry, so there must also ever be bishops in the Church, distinct from the Pope, to govern it. This latter aspect of the episcopate is the express subject of this discussion, the jurisdictional or governing power of the residential bishop while *in office.* We prescind altogether from the canonical procedure of his appointment thereto, and abstract entirely from the possibility of his removal therefrom.

[36] Ottaviani, *Institutiones Iuris Publici Ecclesiastici,* I, n. 211.

PART ONE

THE JURIDICAL STATUS OF THE EPISCOPATE

"Episcopi sunt apostolorum successores atque ex divina institutione peculiaribus ecclesiis praeficiuntur quas cum potestate ordinaria regunt sub auctoritate Romani Pontificis."

—*Canon 329.*

PRELIMINARY REMARKS

The term *juridical status* may perhaps best be explained by distinguishing it from its correlative term, namely juridical function. The latter is merely the authoritative activity of a juridically perfect society. Since, however, social authority is embodied in individual members of the society, juridical function, considered concretely, is the socially authorized activity of particular individuals, that is, according to their official capacity, within the defined scope of their respective official positions. Juridical status is that which determines the *possible* scope of any particular social office.

The scope of any particular social authority is primarily determined by the specific purpose of the official commission for which it is given. Thus, the episcopate in general is intended and *essentially constituted* for the government of the Church, and for that purpose is endowed with the power of jurisdiction. The purpose of individual authorities, however, is itself specified and *existentially characterized* by its relation to the purpose of other authorities in the society. The subordinate episcopate, for example, is intended for the government of a designated diocese, and as such is necessarily modified by the scope of the papal primacy over the universal Church.

The juridical status of any particular social authority, then, or in other words the determinant of its *possible* scope, is merely the aggregate of all those attributes which *essentially constitute* and *existentially characterize* the office or commission to which the authority itself is attached. The concept of juridical status is a synthetic one; it is the result of a fusion of all these attributes into a concept of the *potential capability* of the authority in question. Juridical status, therefore, as distinguished from juridical function (which is a real in the sense of an *actual* entity), though also a real is merely a *potential* entity. It is consequently both the logical and the ontological basis of function, since action depends on and is determined by ability.

It is such a notion which is expressed by the proposition enunciated in canon 329 of the Code of Canon Law. This canon, which aptly introduces that section of the Code which treats of episcopal power, is the latest authoritative and, of those thus far available, the most satisfactory pronouncement on the status of the residential bishop. The content of the canon is all that is materially required from the standpoint of Public Law. It is, moreover, formally so arranged that the sequence of phraseology lends itself without any juxtaposition to a logically progressive commentary of the issue involved.

The following study, therefore, adhering to this natural division of subject-matter, treats in three chapters of the *essential concept,* the *existential character,* and the *potential capability* of the episcopate respectively. To be sure, the summary wording of the canon conveys immediately only the generic canonical import of the theological truth which it embodies. It is suggestive rather than expressive of the specific juridic implications which the incorporation of the canon into the disciplinary code obviously attests. Since these latter are the particular concern of a canonical thesis, they alone are the object of investigation under the above-mentioned headings.

Chapter I

THE ESSENTIAL CONCEPT

"Episcopi sunt apostolorum successores"

The first clause of canon 329 provides a generic definition of the episcopate. It states that bishops are the successors of the apostles. The statement, far from being in any way novel, is merely the expression of the original and persistently traditional concept of the episcopal status. It indicates, first of all, the only legitimate historical foundation for the episcopate, and secondly, its consequent basic juridical prerogatives. The one is signified by the idea of an apostolic succession, the uninterrupted continuance of the apostolic office which because it is historically certain is thereby juridically necessary. The other is contained in the concept of the permanent apostolic status, the substantial identity of the apostolic and episcopal powers. While the statement itself bespeaks expressly only the identity of the apostolate and the episcopate, it obviously supposes the necessary distinction between the two. The following consideration of this concept of apostolic succession and status as the essential notion of the episcopal position in the Church will involve both these aspects, and treat successively of the identity and the disparity of the apostolate and the episcopate.

Article I

Identity of the Apostolate and the Episcopate

Since the ultimate warrant for any permanent apostolic power in the Church depends necessarily on the divinely inspired apostolic intention of a continuance of their office and commission, the historical question concerning the apostolic succession must precede any discussion of the present apostolic status of ecclesiastical authority.

I. Historical Succession

While the Scriptures testify to both the need [1] and the prepara-

[1] Matt. 28: 20.

tion[2] for successors to the apostles, they give no account of the actuality. The need of some *authoritative* succession is a natural consequence of the Church's necessarily prolonged purpose of evangelizing all nations. The need of an *apostolic* succession is demanded by the fact that the apostles were the original rulers of the Church, and it is theologically of faith.[3] The preparation is sufficiently evident in the Scriptural account of the apostolic activity to warrant an *a priori* conclusion as to the fact itself, though there is also ample and conclusive factual evidence, outside the Scriptures, that the traditional was also the earliest concept of the Church's rulers, in the apostolic and immediately post-apostolic Christian society. All the pertinent patristic testimony (beginning with that of St. Clement of Rome, the first and most express witness, whose doctrine the others either explicitly repeat or implicitly suppose) is, as the patrologists and theologians have already conclusively shown, unanimous as to the fact. There were recognized successors to the apostles and they were called bishops, whose power and position, because it was essentially the same, was to be respected no less than that of the apostles themselves.[4] The whole patristic teaching is that the essence of the episcopate is its apostolic descent.

The legitimacy of the Church in its origin, character and personal organization lies in its apostolicity. Christianity after the mind of Christ must indeed ever be essentially apostolic in its doctrine, for the infallible influence of Christ Himself is immanent therein: "Behold I am with you all days, even to the consummation of the world."[5] Moreover, since the Christian faith is a rule of life, true Christianity must also ever be essentially apostolic in its discipline, that is, in following the mind of Christ

[2] Heb. 13:17; Tit. 2:15; I Pet. 5:2; I Thess. 5:12.

[3] Tanquerey, *Synopsis Theologiae Dogmaticae Fundamentalis* (23. ed., Parisiis: Desclée, 1930), nn. 639-642.

[4] St. Clement of Rome, *Ep. ad Cor.* I, 42, 1-4; 44, 1-3—*MPG,* I, 292, 296; St. Irenaeus, *Adv. Haer.,* 3, 3, 1—*MPG,* VII, 848; Tertullian, *De praesc haeret.,* 32—*MPL,* II, 44; Hegesippus, apud Eusebium, *H. E.,* 4, 22—*MPG,* XX, 377.

[5] Matt. 28:20.

as to the manner and the means of perfecting the Redemption which He made possible.

The Church was born on Pentecost; but the intimate relation between the apostolic authority and the Church already appears together with the first evidence of the Church's conception. For Christ first promised authority at the same time as He foretold the establishment of His Church. Peter, an apostle, was first promised it.[6] Later, the other apostles received a promise similar though not identically the same, for Peter was to be the Chief Shepherd of the flock.[7] Christ, faithful to His word, conferred the promised power,[8] and the legitimacy of all ecclesiastical authority depends on the nature of the personal organization which the apostles established as a result. For authority having been first promised and given to the apostles only, *on* one of whom, but *by* all of whom the edifice of Christianity was to be built, the key to the whole structure must lie in the apostolate.

Having commissioned the apostles to teach all nations to observe whatsoever He had commanded, Christ enjoined them to await at Jerusalem the coming of the Holy Ghost.[9] He, the Spirit of Truth, would not only teach them what they did not yet know, but would also remind them of all that Christ had commanded.[10] Consequently, when immediately upon the reception of the Spirit they began to function, it must evidently have been in accord with the suggestion of the Spirit and the will of the Saviour.[11]

[6] Matt. 16:18-19.

[7] Matt. 18:18; John 21:15-17; Luke 22:31.

[8] Matt. 28:18-20; Mark 16:15; John 20:21-23.

[9] Acts 1:4.

[10] John 14:26.

[11] Although forced by historical evidence to admit that Christ gathered to Himself a group of apostles (cf. e.g., Harnack, *Die Mission*, I, 332; Weizsaecker, *Das Apostolische Zeitalter*) and that these apostles formed an organization essentially the same as the Church of today (cf. e.g., Harnack, *Dogmengeschichte*, I, 152, 239, 454) many of the rationalists and liberal theologians of the historical critical school attacked the juridical legitimacy of the Church on the score that it was foreign to the mind of Christ who, they said, intended merely an internal kingdom of the spirit

A synthetic view of the apostolic activity, as opposed to the isolated interpretation of individual texts, demonstrates, as the apologetes scientifically and systematically show that the apostles' divinely guided interpretation of their commission to teach demanded the formation of a society. The earliest account of the Church is that of a community in which there are but two grades of members, the apostles themselves and the multitude. The fellowship of the apostles is the bond of unity, the authority therein.[12] The fact of their superiority is uncontested, its scope unquestioned; and if the community appears more or less as a fraternal union of believers, its behaviour is none the less under a guidance, paternal perhaps in its exercise, but certainly social and jurisdictional in its essence. Though the organization is at first very simple, its authority is from the first sovereign.

It is the apostles, led by Peter, who decide on a substitute for Judas, determine his qualities, confirm his selection and install him in office.[13] Likewise, it was to them that the complaint was made which led them to prescribe the appointment of deacons, to ratify it, and to assign these appointees their duties.[14] They control the common purse, a practice which they had apparently decreed, for Peter pronounces anathema and inflicts the supreme penalty for dishonesty in the matter.[15]

Such in general was the jurisdictional aspect, as gleaned from the Acts of the Apostles, of the infant Church at Jerusalem. The same characteristics are found wherever the winds of persecution dispersed the faithful and their faith, that is to say, first in the surrounding cities of Palestine, and then in the farther sections

based on the bond of moral justice. Cf. Weiss, *Das Unchristentum;* Harnack, *Das Wesen des Christentums,* pp. 34, 92; *Entstehung und Entwicklung der Kirchenverfassung und das Kirchenrechts* (Leipzig, 1910). For an extensive bibliography on this subject from both the Catholic and Protestant viewpoints, cf. Sägmüller, *Lehrbuch des Katholischen Kirchenrechts* (Freiburg im Breisgau: Herder, 1925), pp. 34-35, where the subject is also discussed and unorthodox claims refuted.

[12] Acts 2:42.

[13] Acts 1:15-26.

[14] Acts 6:1-6.

[15] Acts 5:1-10.

of Asia Minor where the Pauline churches flourished. While the records of these latter, in the Acts and in the epistles of St. Paul himself, present a more detailed account of its exercise, the authority to which they attest is fundamentally that which the other apostles had exercised at Jerusalem.[16] Their evidence confirms rather than complements the essentials. Their immediate importance herein springs from their clear testimony as to the separation of the jurisdictional authority from the apostolate proper.

Both the demands of their purely apostolic office and the circumstances occasioned by the numerical growth and the territorial expansion of the faithful rendered the detailed personal supervision employed by the apostles at Jerusalem impossible, and required at least a partial relegation of their power to others. Although after the apostles had left Jerusalem and separated, the individual activity of most of them is for the greater part unknown, the practice of St. Paul, who conformed his procedure to that of the others, must be considered as typical.

Much has been conjectured about the nature of the powers which St. Paul confided to his assistants, with the result that frequently either too little or too much has been proposed concerning it. This much is at least certain, that truly governmental power was conferred in some cases, whatever may have been the corresponding power of Orders (though in some too the fulness of Orders was certainly joined to jurisdiction, as in the persons of Timothy and Titus);[17] and that those who held it did so *ex officio.* Their office was a participation in that of the apostles; for just as St. Peter had called the office lost by Judas *episcopal,* so St. Paul called his appointees *bishops,* and described them as placed by the Holy Ghost, that is, at His divine command, to rule the Church.[18]

The question here, however, is not one of name but one of

[16] Gal. 2:1.

[17] I Tim. 5:22; II Tim. 1:6; Tit. 1:1-10.

[18] Acts 20:28. The word ἐπίσκοπος even among pre-Christian profane authors (e.g., Homer, *Iliad,* 22, 255; *Odyssey,* 8, 163) denoted a public official, and it is so used in the Old Testament (I Mac. 1:51; Ps. 108:8).

fact. In whatever manner the age-old controversy as to names in the early Church may ultimately be settled, the fact is unmistakable almost from the beginning that there existed distinct officials other than the apostles. The apostles had to confer jurisdiction as well as the fulness of Orders. They had to confer Orders on some to insure the continuance of the Sacramental ministry. They had also eventually to confer jurisdiction; and whatever the immediate purpose of those on whom they conferred it, and the precise title by which it was held by them, the power itself was in nature if not in extent apostolic. The ultimate position of these appointees was to be that of successors to the apostles, to provide for the permanent government of the ecclesiastical society.[19] This succession is the basic characteristic of their final and permanent juridical status, as well as of that of all who have since followed them.

This persisted as an unchallenged tenet until the sixteenth century, when the social legitimacy of the Church was first directly attacked and seriously impugned, and on the score of its apostolicity. While this is not a controversial approach to the problem, it may be remarked in answer to all opponents of the present as the primitive Church system (who, while differing among themselves as to the matter at issue, agree on the manner of attack), that the search for essentials cannot be confined to purely Scriptural evidence. The problem, whatever it may be, is not primarily one of textual criticism or comprehensiveness, but one of traditional acceptance, a living tradition older and more complete than the writings, even though inspired, which record it. The latter are not, so to speak, blueprints according to which the Church was constructed, but pictures from which her structural outline can be construed, given her own recognition of the resemblance. Hence, while the New Testament account

[19] II Tim. 4:1-6. "Seniores qui in christianorum coetibus invigilandi munere fungebantur instituti sunt ab Apostolis presbyteri aut episcopi ad providendum necessariae crescentium communitatum ordinationi, non proprie ad perpetuandam missionem et potestatem apostolicam."—Pius X, decret. *"Lamentabili,"* 3 iul. 1907 (propositio Modernistarum damnata 50)—Denzinger-Bannwart, *Enchiridion,* n. 2050.

of her beginning is not complete, it is sufficient assurance of the rest, only because the Church itself antedates the documents, and so she alone can authoritatively authenticate and interpret them. The confusion of these issues has led to critical inferences which are surpassed in absurdity only by the inconsistency of their proponents: the illogical adherence to only some of the basic facts of Christianity, facts so delicately related that by the displacement of one the whole must logically collapse, so that any radical break from the traditional faith should result in its total abandonment.

That of the last century was the most logically consistent of all the heresies, in that from a denial of doctrine and discipline it passed to the denial of Christ's divinity; although it might well lend its name of Protestant Rationalism to all that preceded it or to all that will follow in its wake, especially that of the sixteenth century.[20] For regardless of purpose or progress, all who protest against traditional authority profess an ultimate reliance on individual reason. Such private judgment, however sincere, can only be bad judgment, for the only evidence from which even private judgment can deduce its conclusions is the evidence of history. Moreover, the revision which research and comparative criticism occasion in the history of institutions concerning which there are but few and scanty documents does not extend to manifest facts. The condition of primitive ecclesiology is such that "its history is made up of a few features which, clearly marked from the beginning, acquire with each successive generation a more vigorous and expressive prominence."[21]

[20] The historical problems presented by the attacks on the constitution of the Church, whether by the Reformers, rationalists, or any of the other varied sects, are primarily exegetical or at least apologetical rather than canonical. Consequently, aside from the fact that such attacks have already been conclusively repelled, they are not considered herein, except by passing reference. Cf. in regard to the historical origin of the episcopate and the various claims advanced against its legitimacy, Dunin-Borkowski, *Die neueren Forschungen über die Anfänger des Episkopats* (Freiburg in Brisgovia, 1900).

[21] Batiffol, *Primitive Catholicism* (4. ed., Paris: Gabalda, 1909), p. vi;

Among these certain features the concept of apostolic succession was so prominent a persuasion that for fourteen centuries there is found no direct attack on it even by the authors of heretical sects. The latter, especially Wiclef and Huss, however, not only practically abandoned but moreover so distorted the traditional notion, that they are justly considered the precursors of the sixteenth century reformers. These did not, like the nineteenth century rationalists whom they preceded, deny Christ's divinity and authority to delegate the apostles for their claimed and accepted mission, but either contested the apostolic interpretation of His design and purpose or contended that historical development had substantially voided it of its primitive character. In advancing their theory of a purely invisible Church as the intention of Christ, they denied the very possibility of an apostolic succession as preserved in the episcopate, the traditional authority in the visible society. They had begun by denouncing disciplinary abuse, and proceeding either mistakenly or maliciously to confuse the abuse and the authority which they accused, ended by denying the doctrinal basis of the authority itself. Hence, as indeed consistently with the original integrity of the deposit of faith she could do, in the light of fifteen centuries of episcopal government, the Church was compelled in the Council of Trent (1563) to uphold the episcopate as a juridical institution by means of a solemn definition concerning it.[22]

The Tridentine declaration merely crystallized in doctrinal terms the teaching of centuries, and while the brief statement of the council is not detailed, it contains along with the affirmation of the historical fact also the historically accepted juridical import of the apostolic succession.

"Die Reformation hat, ohne es zu ahnen, Formen modifiziert oder beseitigt, die schon im apostolischen Zeitalter bestandent haben, so . . . in der Verfassung die Bischöfe (und Diakonen)."—Harnack, *Das Wesen des Christentums,* 178.

[22] "Proinde sacrosancta Synodus declarat, praeter ceteros ecclesiasticos gradus *episcopos, qui in Apostolorum locum successerunt,* ad hunc hierarchicum ordinem praecipue pertinere, et 'positos, sicut idem Apostolus ait, a Spiritu Sancto regere Ecclesiam Dei'."—Sess. XXIII, *de ordine,* c. 4—Mansi, XXXIII, 139; Denzinger-Bannwart, *Enchiridion,* n. 960.

II. Juridical Succession.

There is a sense in which all who have any power whatever in the Church are successors to the apostles, in that they participate in either papal or episcopal power which was all originally apostolic. The episcopal successsion, however, is *integral,* that is to say, the episcopote is both materially and formally identical with the apostolate.[23] The material identity of the apostolate and the episcopate denotes that both have substantially the same office, the same commission, the same purpose. The formal identity of the two signifies that both have the same modal prerogatives, the same powers for the accomplishment of the purpose.

For the Fathers the title *bishop* had, at the beginning of the second century,[24] a clearly restricted meaning, as contrasted with its possibly indiscriminate earlier use in the New Testament. It refers to those who have the apostolic power both of Orders and jurisdiction. While there is no mention found in their writings of even a theoretical separability of the two powers, since practically the two were joined in the same personages, the conclusion is not necessarily that all with the fulness of Orders had the equivalent amount of jurisdiction, but on the contrary that all with jurisdiction had the congruous power of Orders.

The issue with which the Council of Trent was concerned was that of a divine warrant for any hierarchy in general as opposed to the universal priesthood of believers.[25] In declaring both the fact of a hierarchy and also the preeminence in the same of bishops who as successors to the apostles are superior to priests, and who are placed by the Holy Spirit to rule the Church of God, the Council, while it most expressly spoke of the power of Orders, nevertheless included without any restrictive distinction both episcopal Orders and jurisdiction; for not only the purely spiritual but even more so the social prerogative of

[23] Schultes, *De Ecclesia Catholica Praelectiones Apologeticae* (Parisiis: Lethielleux, 1931), p. 188.

[24] Ruffini, *La Gerarchia della Chiesa* (Roma: Typographia Pontificia nell'Instituto Pio IX, 1921), p. 16.

[25] I Pet. 2: 5, 9.

the Church had been attacked and required vindication. The terms of dispute, among the doctors of the Council, concerning the immediate origin of jurisdictional authority in the case of the individual bishop, show that the members of the Council, like their predecessors the early Fathers, made little distinction in their discussion between Orders and jurisdiction. Like the Fathers they dealt with a practical system in which the element of jurisdiction was invariably accompanied with the attendant factor of Orders.

Probably to no other topic is the essential distinction between the power of Orders and the power of jurisdiction so important as to that of the episcopate. Though episcopal Orders are not inevitably the mark of episcopal jurisdiction, the latter is usually defined as *the fulness of the Priesthood as established by Christ for the government of the Church*: and a bishop as *one who has received the fulness of the Priesthood as instituted by Christ for the government of the Church.*[26] These statements are rather descriptive of the practice than definitive of the principle, in that they set forth the natural correlation of Orders and jurisdiction, as it appears in both the present and historical custom. They fail, however, to distinguish adequately between the two, and in fact at least imply an essentially necessary merger of the two in the concept of episcopal jurisdiction. The fulness of the Priesthood signifies episcopal Orders, and to define episcopal jurisdiction in terms thereof is to forget the natural distinction in favor of the natural correlation. It is to magnify this correlation from a complementary to a causal one, making the power of Orders inclusive, not only of a particular aptitude for actual, but also of the reality of potential jurisdiction. While the former is admitted, the latter is not warranted. Although Christ united Orders and jurisdiction in the persons of the Apostles, and the positive canon law has habitually required episcopal consecration within a certain time for one promoted to a see, jurisdiction in no wise derives therefrom, and in fact may be fully possessed and exercised without it. The power of Orders, far from being

[26] Bouix, *Tractatus de Episcopo* (2. ed., 2 vols., Parisiis, 1873), I, 91.

generative of jurisdiction, is conditioned upon jurisdictional regulations.[27]

A bishop, then, may be one in episcopal Orders, one with episcopal jurisdiction, or as is generally the case one with both species of ecclesiastical power. Episcopal jurisdiction, moreover, is essentially neither more nor less than the social power instituted by Christ for the government of the Church. It is so because it is the continuance of the apostolic power. As possessed by the successors of the apostles, however, while substantially the same as the apostolic prerogative, it is necessarily somewhat different. This difference appears from a consideration of the disparity between the apostolate and the episcopate.

Article II

Disparity of the Apostolate and the Episcopate

The apostles themselves enjoyed a double status. They were at once the immediate, though instrumental, authors of the Church and the accredited authorities within it. Their office or commission was first of all to found the Church according to Christ's plan, and having laid the foundation to rule it according to that plan. Their position was unique, and on the strength of it theologians have always distinguished in their persons a twofold office, the apostolate proper or their status as Christ's

[27] Cavagnis in discussing whether the jurisdiction of the collegiate episcopate in ecumenical council takes its origin from the Pope directly or from episcopal consecration, says as to the latter possibility: " . . . hinc inutiliter supponitur a Deo collata actu jurisdictio in Ecclesiam universalem, quae nequit exerceri [i.e., outside of council], sed jurisdictio quae actu habeatur et non modo illicite sed invalide exerceatur intelligi nequit. Est enim jurisdictio ius gubernativum personarum, seu ius imperandi seu obligandi; iamvero imperium invalidum est imperium datum sine iure obligandi; quod est contradictorium. Sed huiusmodi esset jurisdictio episcopalis . . . particularis absque designatione dioecesis regendae. Ergo non est dicendum episcopis [i.e., those in episcopal orders] competere jurisdictionem, sed eos esse in eo gradu qui *completum* constituit subjectum ut recipiat jurisdictionem eamque exerceat *convenienter,* et per personas huius gradus Ecclesiam *normaliter* regi, ideoque gradui generice esse debitam."—*Institutiones Iuris Publici Ecclesiastici,* I. 461.

instruments in establishing the ecclesiastical society, and the episcopate or their standing as rulers in it.[28] The relation between these two official positions of the apostles is so intimate that their commission to found the Church lent a peculiar prerogative to their government of it.

To understand the exact nature of this relationship a further distinction must be made between the apostolate as exemplified in Peter alone and as represented in the other members of the apostolic college. The Church was built *by* all but *on* one. Peter was not only a founder of the Church, but the very foundation itself.[29] His foundational function must last as long as the Church lasts, while the constructive agency of the others ceased when the structure was completed. Hence, since the purely apostolic mission of Peter perdured, the prerogative which it lent to his governing power or jurisdiction also persisted and was transferred to his successors in office. In the case of the others, on the contrary, this special characteristic ceased with its cause and was not continued in their successors.

The characteristic of the apostolic power referred to here is the *universality* of jurisdiction enjoyed by the apostles, not only collectively but also individually. The entire and precise import of this prerogative of the apostolic jurisdiction can at most be merely surmised. It was certainly not equal to that of Peter, but by its nature was subordinate to his universal authority, and in its use dependent thereon.[30] The apostles other than Peter did not singly have universal jurisdiction in the sense that they could, for example, legislate for the whole Church, except of course by divine revelation; in this latter instance, however, the laws

[28] Billot, *Tractatus de Ecclesia Christi*, p. 231.

[29] Matt. 16:13-19.

[30] "Inter ceteros Apostolos eminebat Petrus, qui plena potestate legisfera indutus erat in universam Ecclesiam. Singuli tamen Apostoli potestatem quodammodo universalem et ipsi obtinebant: at duplicem restrictionem patiebatur eorum auctoritas: 1) Petrum ligare non poterant, bene vero eos Petrus; 2) suis Ecclesiis a se fundatis leges imponere poterant, non autem toti Ecclesiae independenter a Petro."—Rivet, *Institutiones Iuris Ecclesiastici Privati* (Romae, 1914), p. 15; cf. Wernz, *Ius Decretalium* (2. ed., 6 vols., Prati, 1905-1915), I, n. 91.

were divine and not merely apostolic. Whatever was the scope and efficacy of this universality of apostolic power, the prerogative itself was but temporary and transient in the case of all but Peter in whom it was essentially the same as it has been ever since in his successors, the Bishops of Rome. Consequently, there is no real juridic need for speculation regarding its meaning for the other apostles. The continuation of the extraordinary apostolic powers cannot be proved historically, and it is positively denied on dogmatic grounds as the words of Pius VI clearly demonstrate.[31]

The authority of Peter to establish and to rule the Church in the world as a whole was ordinary, official and communicable. His universal jurisdiction passed to his successors. The power of the rest of the apostles to establish the Church throughout the world was, on the other hand, extraordinary, personal to them and inalienable. Consequently, the universality of jurisdiction which it carried with it ended therewith, though the jurisdiction itself, the purely gubernatorial power, could be, because it had to be, transmitted to others, its purpose being the continued government of the enduring society.[32] That is to say, their jurisdiction in itself was also ordinary, official and communicable.[31]

The jurisdiction to which bishops succeed, then, is not precisely equal to that of the apostles, but similar thereto.[32] There are two main points of distinction between the power of the apostles and that of the bishops who succeed them. The first is a difference in official status and the second is a difference in

[31] "*Dogma catholicum est,* Apostolos, tametsi extraordinaria praeditos potestate, quae data personis cum ipsis personis interiit, fuisse Petro subjectos, quem solum Apostolis praeesse Christus iussit: et subesse plenitudini potestatis Romani Pontificis (quae veluti ordinaria in Petro, ita in eius successoribus ordinaria est) omnes *Episcopos, qui extraordinaria potestate Apostolorum destituuntur.*" *Responsio super Nunciaturis Apostolicis* (Romae: 1789), c. 9, I, p. 300.

[32] Pius X, decret. "*Lamentabili,*" 4 iul. 1907 (prop. damnat. 50)—Denzinger-Bannwart, *Enchiridion,* n. 2050.

[33] Billot, *Tractatus de Ecclesia Christi,* I, 546.

[34] Bouix, *Tractatus de Episcopo,* I, 53-54.

jurisdictional extent. The bishops, first of all, have only a single official status as compared to that of the apostles which was twofold. The status of bishops, as St. Paul declared[35] and the Council of Trent defined, is that of rulers of the Church of God, whereas that of the apostles was that of instrumental founders as well as rulers of the Church. Whereas the apostles as the immediate instruments of Christ proposed new revelations of doctrine and decreed new dispositions of discipline as the basis of the new spiritual dispensation, it is the duty of their successors, the bishops, to guard without substantial change the deposit of doctrine and to enforce the system of discipline which they have received from the apostles.[36] As St. Augustine said of those who preceded him in the apostolic succession: they held to that which they found, they taught that which they learnt, and that which they accepted from the Fathers they passed on to their sons.[37]

The second distinguishing feature of episcopal jurisdiction in the successors of the apostles is that it is juridically limited as to locality.[38] This limitation entails more than merely local restriction in the sense that within their territorial boundaries the successors of the apostles are jurisdictionally unrestricted. For, as will be seen, this local limitation is consequent to the fundamental purpose of the episcopate and involves a further material subordination and actual dependence, since it radically affects the jurisdictional power as a distinct juridical institute coordinate to the papal primacy.

The distinction between the apostolate and the episcopate in Peter himself was and can ever be (in his successors) merely virtual; and although it was a real distinction in the rest of the apostolic college, it appears as merely potential in their persons.

[35] Acts 20:28.

[36] II Tim. 2:2; 3:10, 14; 13:14; Pesch, *Praelectiones Theologicae* (3. ed., 9 vols., Friburgi Brisgoviae, 1903), I, n. 435.

[37] "Quod invenerunt in ecclesia, tenuerunt, quod didicerunt, docuerunt, quod a patribus acceperunt, hoc filiis tradiderunt."—*Contra Julian,* 2, 10, 34—*MPL, XLIV,* 698.

[38] Tit. 1:5-6; I Tim. 3:1 ss.

It was actualized only when they associated others to themselves in their work, and when the *episcopal* office acquired its present *name.* As a distinct office from the apostolate itself, the episcopate did not immediately receive the *form* which it now has. The so-called monarchic episcopate does not appear definitely in the evidence available as to the *immediate separation* of the apostolate and the episcopate. It does, however, manifest itself in the *ultimate succession* of the episcopate to the apostolic office, and it then appears as a primary and preserved existential feature of the juridical succession.

Chapter II

THE EXISTENTIAL CHARACTER

"Atque ex divina institutione peculiaribus ecclesiis praeficiuntur"

This second clause of canon 329 expresses directly the traditional form, and indirectly insinuates the juridical tenure of episcopal jurisdiction. Obviously the clause in question is a description of the present system of Church polity in the subordinate field. For while it explicitly states that bishops are assigned to particular churches, that is, to dioceses, there is no insinuation of a double or collegiate diocesan authority in the use of the plural expression. Any doubt is precluded by the tenor of the whole tract introduced by this canon. The form is usually called monarchic. That term, however, signifies a personal prerogative rather than a personal pattern. The two questions are, indeed, closely connected, but are not precisely identical. The form or pattern might indeed be monarchic in the sense that only one bishop is set over a diocese, without his tenure being monarchic in the sense that he alone, radically at least, rules the diocese. To distinguish these two questions, it may perhaps be preferable to refer to the form as unitary, and the tenure as monarchic.

Article I

Unitary Form of the Residential Episcopate

In discussing the unitary form of the subordinate episcopate, care must be taken to distinguish the question of fact from the question of law. The former is the historical and the latter the juridical basis of the system.

I. Factual Question.

To say that the beginnings of the episcopate in its present and long-traditional form are both obscure and obvious is no paradox, but a paramount fact in its history. The traditional idea by which the unity of the Universal Church is to be reflected in each part thereof has established the unitary episcopate as the regular and most perfect form, and as an incontestable principle of diocesan government.[1]

The unitary episcopate is the system in which 1) only one bishop presides over any particular diocese, and 2) a bishop presides over one diocese only. There is little legislation on either of these points, the first of which is by far the more fundamental. The Council of Nice (325) provided for the reinstatement of the returning penitent Novatian bishops in accordance with this unitary idea.[2] The first Council of Constantinople (381) "accepts and develops the Nicene legislation as to the territorial arrangements of the ecclesiastical Hierarchy,"[3] by restricting the bishops to their own peculiar territory.[4] Again, though much later, the Fourth Council of the Lateran (1215) definitely forbade the practice whereby more than one bishop would rule a see, saying that such a condition would be as monstrous as that of one body having two heads.[5] The Council of Trent (1547) proscribed the converse of this, the holding of several sees by one bishop.[6] There is nothing radical in these enactments. They are merely expressive of the accepted tradition against particular instances of abuse. However, it has long been a question as to the exact origin and the precise basis of the unitary policy.

The Nicene legislation quoted above shows that the system was the only admitted practice at the beginning of the fourth century. The Council of Nice, however, did not inaugurate the practice.

[1] Ruffini, *La Gerarchia della Chiesa,* p. 21.

[2] Canon 8: " . . . ne in civitate duo sint episcopi."—Mansi, II, 671.

[3] Schroeder, *Disciplinary Decrees of the General Councils* (St. Louis: B. Herder, 1937), p. 64.

[4] Canon 2: "Secundum regulas, constitutus Alexandriae quidem Episcopus, ea quae sunt in Aegypto tantum gubernet."—Mansi, III, 557.

[5] "Prohibemus autem omnino, ne una eademque civitas sive dioecesis diversos Pontifices habeat, tanquam unum corpus diversa capita, quasi monstrum."—Cap. IX, *Quoniam, de officio judicis ordinarii.*—Mansi, XXII, 998.

[6] "Nemo quacumque etiam dignitate, gradu, aut praeeminentia praefulgens, plures metropolitanas seu cathedrales ecclesias, in titulum, sive commendam, aut alio quovis nomine, contra sacrorum canonum instituta recipere et simul retinere praesumat."—Sess. VII. *de ref.,* c. 2—Mansi, XXXIII, 50.

St. Cyprian, for example, testifies that it was the rule at the middle of the third century.[7] Indeed, it is unanimously admitted that the system was universal at the end of the second century.[8] Furthermore, it is apparent from the writings of St. Ignatius of Antioch, who died about the year 107, that the unitary was at least the usual form of local administration before the beginning of the second century.[9] In each of the local churches to which he writes there is but one bishop. Ignatius is the first intentional witness of the system, and his account is the more valuable in that what he is consciously championing is not a unitary as opposed to a collegiate episcopate, but rather ecclesiastical discipline as against heresy and schism. He does not speak of the unitary form as a novelty, nor as peculiar to the churches which he addresses, but as the only form with which he himself is acquainted.[10] His testimony is ample and conclusive proof of the character of the local organization of his day; for the policy which he describes, if not the only, was certainly the characteristic one, and became, as has been said, by the beginning of the third century the one recognized discipline, preserved thenceforth to the present, as all subsequent evidence both doctrinal and practical demonstrates.[11]

However, although the fact of the unitary system is almost a truism from the time of Ignatius, there is still considerable doubt and difference of opinion concerning the time prior to that in which he wrote. The real historical question, as opposed to the historical certainty summarized above, is due to the gap between the Ignatian and the Pauline epistles, a lacuna which at

[7] "Singulis pastoribus portio gregis adscripta est, quam regat unusquisque et gubernet."—*Ep. 65 ad Cornelium Papam*—*MPL*, IV, 332.

[8] Batiffol, *Primitive Catholicism*, p. 405.

[9] Textual examples of the Ignatian teaching will be found under the following article on the monarchic tenure, to which they most explicitly attest.

[10] *Ep. ad Eph.*, III, 2: " . . . ut et episcopi, *per tractus terrae* constituti, in sententia Jesu Christi sunt."—*MPG*, V, 648.

[11] E.g., St. Bernard (1153): "Habent illi [i.e., episcopi] sibi assignatos greges, *singuli singulos;*" " . . . alii singuli singulos sortiti sunt plebes." —*De Consideratione*, II, 8, ad Eugenium Papam—*MPL*, CLXXXII, 752.

most can be stretched to cover a period of fifty years. During that time a change seems to have taken place with so little disturbance that it has left no trace at all in historical record. For except during the very temporary intervals when Timothy and Titus as apostolic delegates were in charge of the church at Ephesus and Crete respectively, what evidence there is of the Pauline churches discloses a collegiate body at the head of the local communities,[12] while the Ignatian writings take for granted the unitary system. Various attempts have been made to reconcile these apparent extremes. The issue seems to have been somewhat confused by the lack of not only possible, but necessary distinctions. The assumption, first of all, that every local community of the apostolic era enjoyed the autonomy of the present day diocese is altogether unwarranted. Nor, in the second place, is it proper to conclude that there was an evolution in the notion of the unitary system simply because there is evidence of a numerical growth of unitary superiors. The origin and the multiplication of the unitary episcopate are two distinct questions, the multiplication indeed, is still going on, and there are yet many regions where the system has not been instituted, and which the Pople rules by Vicars and Prefects Apostolic.

The origin of the unitary form, however, is definitely relegated to the apostolic epoch, before the death of St. John, the last surviving apostle about the year 100. A well-founded tradition has it that during the last years of his life St. John established the unitary episcopate in several churches of Asia Minor, among them those mentioned in the Apocalypse.[13] For despite all that has been written to the contrary, the old interpretation, which views the angels as the individual bishops of the seven churches, still seems to be the most satisfactory,[14] especially since several of the churches named are among those addressed by Ignatius.[15]

[12] Acts 20:28; Michiels, *De Origine Episcopatus* (Louvain: 1900), pp. 277-278.

[13] Eusebius, *H. E.*, 3, 23, 6-7—*MPG*, XX, 270.

[14] Apoc. 1:4; Simon-Prado, *Praelectiones Biblicae* (3. ed., 2 vols., Taurini: Marietti, 1930), II, n. 971.

[15] I.e., Ephesus, Smyrna, Philadelphia.

St. Irenaeus (160-200), who, incidentally, witnesses the fact of the unitary episcopate in all the churches during his time, specifically, as does also Tertullian,[16] testifies to St. Polycarp's appointment to the see of Smyrna by St. John the Apostle.[17] Elsewhere, Tertullian speaks of the disciple-churches of the Apocalypse, and of St. John as their founder.[18]

This is the most definite evidence available regarding the actual early appointment of individual bishops as the superiors of the local churches by the apostles, and some contend that since it is in connection with him that it first explicitly appears St. John was the author of the unitary system.[19] The one certain conclusion from this evidence is that during St. John's lifetime there were individual bishops at the head of local communities, and that he appointed some of them. One cannot say that they did not priorly exist, merely because they happen to appear definitely only during his time. Indeed, the position of St. James at Jerusalem militates against the assertion.[20]

Though the personal identity of the latter is sometimes controverted, the question is purely of historical interest, and not of juridic import.[21] There is little occasion to believe he was other than one of the original twelve apostles. There is certainly no room at all for doubt concerning his official status, as gleaned from the Acts and confirmed by tradition. He was a person of singular importance, to whom Peter announced his delivery from prison, who after Peter is foremost in the Council of Jerusalem in the year 51, who send legates to Antioch, to whom Paul hastens to report,[22] and whom, finally, Clement of Alexandria calls bishop of Jerusalem.[23] It would, therefore, appear that the

[16] *De praescr.*, 32—*MPL,* II, 44.

[17] *Adv. Haer.*, 3, 3, 4—*MPG,* VII. 851.

[18] *Adv. Marc.*, 4, 5—*MPL,* II, 366.

[19] Moran, *The Government of the Church in the First Century* (New York: Benziger, 1913), pp. 251-254.

[20] Michiels, *De Originie Episcopatus,* pp. 233-247.

[21] Ruffini, *La Gerarchia della Chiesa,* p. 31.

[22] Acts 12:17; Gal. 2:12; Acts 15:6-21; 21:17, 18.

[23] Eusebius, *H. E., 2,* 1—*MPG,* XX, 135.

unitary episcopate is not only apostolic in its origin, as to point of time, but also in its title as well, at least in the case of one apostle.

Furthermore, though St. James is the only apostle whose position exactly resembles that of the modern residential bishop, that of the others of whom we have knowledge may also be construed in a similar light. Though their jurisdiction was in some sense universal, St. Paul himself is a witness to their practice of not building on another's foundation.[24] This implies, at least, that ordinarily they restricted themselves to the government of that area which they had themselves evangelized and organized.[25] However, while it is in regard to the Pauline churches that the indication of a collegiate government of the local communities arises, as for instance at Ephesus, the status of the officials collegiate must not be overestimated.

Much has been conjectured as to the precise nature of their authority. "In the church of the Apostles, because of the tremendous authority of the Apostles, each of whom directed the Church he had newly founded, the local elders of the individual Churches were so overshadowed that on purely historical grounds we cannot even accurately determine the scope of their office."[26] Certainly it was jurisdictional, and so essentially episcopal. In fact, as has been said, the name arose from St. Paul's use of it in his allocution to the elders of Ephesus. They were placed as *bishops to rule*.[27] The power which these officials held, however, was not episcopal power as it exists today. For the first transmission of power by the apostles was not to successors as such, but to auxiliaries.[28] It must be remembered that while they lived

[24] Rom. 15:20.

[25] Ruffini, *La Gerarchia della Chiesa*, p. 28.

[26] Koesters, *The Church, Its Divine Authority* (Translation from the German by Rev. Edwin Kaiser, C.PP.S., St. Louis: B. Herder, 1938), p. 212.

[27] Acts 20:28. The Greek *ποιμάινειν* literally signifies to tend, as a flock, but since the flock is the Church, a society, the power of management is truly social or jurisdictional. Cf. Simon-Prado, *Praelectiones Biblicae*, I, 65, n. 529.

[28] Ruffini, *La Gerarchia della Chiesa*, p. 26.

the apostles themselves retained the supreme control and authority over the church which they had founded.[29] They entrusted to others only the immediate regulation of the individual communities. The authority, indeed, resided in the office of the appointees. It was, therefore, ordinary power. The local units of the Church themselves ruled by these officials were, it seems, not as yet (that is, during the lifetime of the apostles) the autonomous divisions that they were eventually to become. The power of those who immediately ruled them, though ordinary, seems not to have been proper, but vicarious, held as it was in the name of the apostle, who did not confide his alienable governing power in full, but only partially. He himself continued to have the care of all the churches.[30] Although his diocese was of much greater extent than is now customary, he was personally the supreme superior over it.[31] However, because he was unable to do so personally, he frequently exercised his authority over both the stationary officials and their subjects by the appointment of itinerant delegates such as Timothy and Titus.[32]

The jurisdiction conferred on both these types of assistants, precisely because it was not the highest local authority, was, therefore, not episcopal in either its extent or its intensity, and far less superepiscopal as some would suggest,[33] but rather infraepiscopal, akin by nature to that of the present day diocesan officials who assist the bishop. Although it may have been more extensive than that of these present day officials, and was possibly relatively as extensive as episcopal authority today, still it was neither as extensive nor as intensive as that of the apostles, who themselves were alone the bishops proper and the highest territorial supervisors. For the relation of the other apostles to Peter was essentially the same, though not so practically evidenced, as that of the modern bishop to the Roman Pontiff, and the lesser authori-

[29] Tanquerey, *Synopsis Theologiae Dogmaticae Fundamentalis,* n. 646.

[30] I Cor. 5:3; 13:10.

[31] Ruffini, *La Gerarchia della Chiesa,* p. 90.

[32] II Tim. 4:10-11; Tit. 1:5; Michiels, *De Origine Episcopatus,* pp. 249-251.

[33] Moran, *The Government of the Church in the First Century,* p. 163.

ties must correspond accordingly. One must beware of trying to fit each individual original community and its officials too closely into the pattern which shortly afterward, in the latter days of St. John began to take shape, and which has since remained fundamentally the same.

The scriptural account of the Church's organization closes while, in the person of St. John at least, the juridic personality of the apostolic college itself was still extant. The account, therefore, makes no mention of the actual succession. The activity of St. John prepared for it, and was directed to the erection of smaller divisions of local administration for the purpose of efficiency and solidarity immediately, and diocesan autonomy ultimately, though not until the succession occurred.

The process is still witnessed in the division of an already existing diocese into several smaller ones. The later appearance, then, in primitive ecclesiology of a single bishop where a college once ruled may perhaps best be construed as a change in the character of the district itself rather than the sign of a change in the status of its *highest local* (as distinguished from universal or papal) government. Thus far it has been ruled by a college (whether composed of officials in episcopal or sacerdotal orders makes no difference in the matter of jurisdiction) as vicars of the apostles. It has been thus far a kind of diocesan vicariate, though ordained to ultimate diocesan autonomy. When, therefore, these communities next appear in historical record with a single bishop governing them, it is because the community itself has ceased to be such a vicariate, and has attained the independence of a diocese. The apostles have died, and the ordinary power has ceased to be vicarious and has become proper and the bishop governs not as distinct from the former college, but as distinct from the apostle whom he succeeded, and who had previously ruled the community in question as *part* of his own proper flock.

The apostles themselves were individual superiors; one of them at least, St. John, provided for individual successors to himself in the churches over which he presided and continued to preside to a greater or lesser extent until his death. The legitimate presumption from this evidence is that the same occurred elsewhere. In the lack of documentary testimony against this hypothesis the burden of proof would seem to rest on those who contest it. For although the apostles for some reason or other may have permitted the one or the other community (not yet a diocese in the proper sene) to be governed by a college, the collegiate officials do not appear precisely as actual *successors* to the apostles who are still alive and in whom alone the episcopate proper exists, or (while St. John survived alone) in their juridic representative.

The succession itself was not completely accomplished until the death of the last apostle, and that is time enough to look for the personal pattern thereof. The successors were, indeed, to be found among the apostolic appointees, but there is no evidence that the jurisdictional episcopate was to devolve upon all equally. On the contrary, when successors as such first appear in history as jurisdictional superiors, in the letters of St. Ignatius written within a few years of the end of the apostolate, they appear as individual authorities in the local churches which were wholely developed, even if not in the undeveloped mission stations.

II. Juridical Question.

The unitary episcopate, then, is a present juridical fact with a primitive and uninterrupted historical foundaton.[34] In the past, however, authors have discussed the theoretical possibility of both a collegiate government in a single see, and the converse question of a single episcopal authority over several sees.[35] As has been said, the former of these is the more important question. The latter situation does no essential violence to the unitary system, for the bishop is still the unique superior in each of the dioceses

[34] Conc. Vat., Sess. IV, c. 3: "Episcopi, qui positi a Spiritu Sancto in Apostolorum locum successerunt, tanquam veri pastores assignatos sibi greges, *singuli singulos, pascunt et regunt* . . . "—Denzinger-Bannwart, *Enchiridion,* n. 1828; "Usu namque etiam ab Ecclesiae incunabulis receptum est, ut ceteris ecclesiis *singuli* Episcopi praeficiantur."—Natalis Alexander, *Historia Ecclesiastica* (11 vols., Venetiis: Gatti, 1778-1793), IV, Dissert. 44 in Saeculum IV.

[35] Bouix, *Tractatus de Episcopo,* I, 315.

over which he presides. There are numerous enough examples throughout history of this possibility, which is still admitted by the Code.[36] There are, on the other hand, no instances of the former, and in addition to the positive legislation of the general councils quoted above, there are examples of particular councils legislating on the same point. Thus, the Council of Carthage (419) made rather minute regulations concerning the bishops converted from Donatism, among others that the provision of dioceses among them should be made so that only one bishop would govern a single territory, and that the territories be so divided as to provide for this.[37]

There are, indeed, several historical instances of two bishops ruling the same locality, whose jurisdiction was of the same local extent, but whose respective authorities extended to different subjects within the territory, by reason of the material difference in rite and language,[38] even as now in the case of Latins and Orientals. In such cases where greater utility is had for the faith, it is indisputably admitted that several bishops may be appointed to one and the same district, but to different material objects within it.[39] The unitary system is not essentially derogated thereby.

However, despite the constant practice and the consistent postive legislation in favor of the unitary form of episcopal government, there is still considerable dispute as to the exact juridical warrant for it. There can be no doubt that it was apostolic in origin as to point of time. Nor is there any evidence that it was of other than apostolic instrumentality in its direct instituton. The question remains, however, as to whether the apostles, in instituting it or allowing it to begin, acted on their own or on divine authority. Some claim that it was the former, and that consequently the unitary system is of ecclesiastical law, and took its initiative from

[36] Canon 339, § 5.

[37] *Codex Canonum Ecclesiae Africanae*, canons 117, 118—Mansi, III, 815-818.

[38] Benedict XIV, *De Synodo Dioecesana*, lib. 2, c. 12, n. 6.

[39] Benedict XIV, *De Synodo Diocesana*, lib. 13, c. 10, n. 29.

the practical necessity of a president in the earlier collegiate assemblies.[40] The clause which expresses the system in the Code, however, is introduced by a phrase[41] which seems to establish the latter, although some regard the phrase as not too well chosen.[42] The legislator bases the fact on *divine institution.* The interpretation offered above concerning the status of the apostles themselves as unitary superiors would seem to confirm this. It is a grave matter, and not likely to have been left to the arbitrary decision of the apostles.

It is quite true that the fact to which the legislator attributes divine instiution may be that of the necessity of episcopal government in the Church generally, as that fact follows from the fact of the apostolic succession. This point, however, is amply enunciated in the previous clause of the canon, and there is no need for repetition. It seems preferable, therefore, to interpret the phrase in question as directly applicable to the particular implications of the clause which it introduces. Thus, in the first place, it would refer to the unitary system of episcopal government, and might well be taken as an indication of an evolution in the dogmatic concept of the apostolic succession, in view of the historical background. It would equivalently emphasize the immediate consequence of this, the radical need for territorial divisions of the Church. This last is, indeed, immediately derived only from apostolic institution; for there is no evidence of Christ's having commanded it explicitly. However, it must be fundamentally attributed to divine ordinance, since it is a necessary complement of the Church's organization.[43]

[40] Batiffol, *Études d'histoire et de théologie positive* (Paris, 1920), p. 271: "Pour nous . . . l'épiscopat est antérieur au moment où il devient monarchique, et seule cette qualité de monarchique est d'initiative ecclésiastique."

[41] Canon 329, § 1: " . . . *ex divina institutione* peculiaribus ecclesiis praeficiuntur . . . "

[42] Augustine, *A Commentary on the New Code of Canon Law,* II, 342.

[43] "De essentia episcopatus ideoque *iuris divini* non est *dioecesis* proprie dicta i.e. certum ac praefinitum territorium. Proinde singuli episcopatus, cum eorum territorio et sede, sunt *iuris humani* . . . Confundenda non

It is difficult to see how the episcopal office can be a practical factor in the government of the Church without territorially separated jurisdictions. There must be bishops by divine command to continue the apostolic office; and however small a number of them would satisfy this necessity, they would have to function collegiately if there were no local distinctions for each, and if confusion and discord, not to say contradictory ordinances, were to be avoided. The power of their successors, however, is not merely collegiate any more than was that of the apostles themselves. How then, without individual local assignments, would it be humanly feasible for them to function individually? The Church, though spiritual and divinely directed, is nevertheless largely left to human instrumentality.

Territorial divisions do not indeed postulate a unitary episcopate since a collegiate body is quite conceivable in each territory. The unitary episcopate, however, does postulate territorial distinctions. The latter follow logically from the former, just as they did chronologically. For the apostles were individual authorities not because there had priorly existed particular and determined localities to which they were severally assigned, but because they chose different fields of labor. It would appear that they did so because it was implied in the divine command to teach all nations, since only by separation could they begin to reach such bounds.

The apostles established the division of the Universal Church. They established it, however, as a fact to be followed, not as an unalterable pattern. For though the fact itself may have been directly ordered by divine decree, the particular boundaries were certainly the work of the apostles themselves. Consequently the Sovereign Pontiff can alter the territorial pattern according to expediency. Moreover, the necessity of episcopal government in the Church and, as it would appear, its exercise in the unitary

est dioecesis proprie dicta, scil. certum et praefinitum territorium secundum hodiernum conceptum, cum *particulari Ecclesia,* seu certa ac determinata fidelium portione ab Episcopo regenda. Haec *iuris divini* dicenda."—Cappello, *Summa Iuris Canonici* (2. ed., 3 vols., Romae: Apud Aedes Universitatis Gregorianae, 1932), I, 440; Ottaviani, *Institutiones Iuris Publici Ecclesiastici,* I, 463.

form,[44] do not require that the whole territorial expanse of the world be so governed, but that it be the usual and perfect form, to which others, such as vicariates and prefectures apostolic, should be, as they in fact are, ultimately ordained.[45] This does not mean that there must be a progressive multiplication of territorial divisions in the Church ruled by individual residential bishops. Changing conditions may render small dioceses more efficient at one time and centralization more expedient at another. Consequently, the unison of existent dioceses into fewer, rather than their division into more, or the change of a diocese into a vicariate or the like, may be followed as long as there are sufficient divisions to satisfy the divine command for a number of monarchic bishops in the government of the Church.

Article II

Monarchic Tenure of the Residential Episcopate

As was explained above, the question of the monarchic tenure of episcopal government differs from the foregoing question concerning the unitary form thereof.[46] It is, however, a necessary consequence of the preceding conclusions. For since the bishops alone are the divinely instituted jurisdictional successors of the apostles, it follows that, if there is by divine ordinance only one of them in a given diocese, the official power of the diocese is *radically* entirely resident in his person. The question of monarchic tenure, then, is the question of the bishop's relation to other authorities existent with the diocese. It may be examined historically and juridically.

I. Historical Basis.

There can be no doubt that the apostles themselves, as the original bishops, were radically the monarchic superiors over the churches which they had founded. They associated others to them-

[44] Bolgeni, *L'Episcopato* (2. ed., 2 vols., Orvieto, 1837), I, 219.

[45] Bouix, *Tractatus de Episcopo*, I, 82-83.

[46] "La question diffère de la précédente, car l'évêque pourrait être unique sans avoir pour cela pleine autorité dans son dioecese."—Prat, "Évêques,"—*Dictionnaire de Théologie Catholique*, V, 1656-1701.

selves as sharers in their jurisdiction. These participants, however, derived their authority entirely from the apostles, and their participation in the apostolic power did not in any way lessen the actual authority in its original source, the persons of the apostles. It was not a division of power but a duplication of persons participating in the same power, since the apostles retained both potentially and actually authority equivalent to and beyond that which was committed to others. The historical question, however, is whether or not their successors were likewise endowed with this monarchic quality. Here again it must be remembered that one cannot argue as to the characteristics of the apostolic succession precisely from the conditions which may have characterized the government of the local churches during the lifetime of the apostles. These latter were not dioceses, but apostolic vicariates, and their immediate officials were the apostolic vicars or delegates, whether stationary or itinerant.

When successors as such first appear in historical record, that is, in the writings of St. Ignatius of Antioch mentioned above, they are not only individual superiors of their flocks, but are possessed of a definitely monarchic prerogative. In all the churches to which he directs his letters there is but one bishop, union with whom in doctrine is the only assurance of the truth, obedience to whom it all matter of ecclesiastical discipline is the authentic mark of a christian.[47] Ignatius, indeed, witnesses the existence of other authorities in the local church. He generally mentions the priests and deacons, but there is no question of the difference he recognized between them and the bishop.[48]

[47] *Ep. ad Eph.*, V, 3: "Studeamus igitur episcopo non resistere ut simus subjecti Deo."—*MPG*, V, 648; *Ep. ad Trall.*, II, 2: "Necessarium itaque est, quemadmodum facitis, ut sine episcopo nihil agatis."—*MPG*, V, 676; *Ep. ad Polyc.*, IV, 1: "Nihil sine tua voluntate fiat . . . "—*MPG*, V, 723; *Ep. ad Magnes.*, XIII, 1: Subjecti estote episcopo . . . ut Jesus Christus Patri."—*MPG*, V, 673; *Ep. ad Smyrn.*, VIII, 1: " . . . separatim ab episcopo nemo quidquam faciat eorum quae ad ecclesiam spectant."—*MPG*, V, 713.

[48] *Ep. ad Trall.*, XII: "Decet enim singulos vestrum et *praecipue presbyteros*, refocillare Episcopum, in honorem Patris, Jesu Christi, et Apostolorum."—*MPG*, V, 799.

St. Cyprian, likewise, not only testifies to the unitary system but also to the monarchic quality of episcopal government.[49] As theologians and apologetes have amply demonstrated, these are not isolated texts, their tenor is found in all the patristic literature. It suffices herein to quote these few as evidence that the monarchic characteristic was as fundamentally recognized from the beginning as that of the unitary form.

The same is evident also from the early conciliar legislation. Thus, the Council of Ancyra (314),[50] the Council of Laodicea[51] and the First Council of Toledo (400),[52] all witness the superiority of the bishop over the priests of the diocese in particular, and since the latter were and are admittedly the next ranking participants in ecclesiastical power, all lesser authorities are equivalently, though implicitly, subordinated to the bishop. The original tradition is unanimous concerning the monarchic episcopate, and was not contested until the fourth century when Aërius denied the superiority of bishops to priests. This heresy which St. Epiphanius calls the worst of all since the beginning,[53] though originally short-lived, was substantially revived in the sixteenth century by Calvin, and to some extent in the eighteenth century by the Synod of Pistoia.

Aërius admitted that historically until his day the bishops were the jurisdictional superiors of the priests, but denied that they were so by divine right. It would appear that his error was due first of all to a misconception of the power of Orders as equal in both bishop and priest. It resulted secondly from a con-

[49] "Inde per temporum et successionum vices Episcoporum ordinatio et Ecclesiae ratio decurrit, ut Ecclesia super Episcopos constituatur, et *omnis actus Ecclesiae per eosdem praepositos gubernetur."—Ep. 27—MPL,* IV, 298.

[50] Canon 12: "Non liceret presbyteris civitatis sine praecepto Episcopi vel litteris in unaquaque Parochia aliquid imperare."—Mansi, II, 532.

[51] Canon 57: "Presbyteros nihil agere debere sine mente Episcopi."—Mansi, II, 590. The exact date of this council is uncertain. Some authors place it as early as 314, others as late as 399.

[52] Canon 20: "Sine conscientia episcopi presbyteri nihil agere praesumant."—Mansi, III, 1002.

[53] *Adv. Haer.*, LXXV,—*MPG,* XLII, 503.

fusion of Orders and jurisdiction, which he considered so coordinate as to be mutually equivalent so that since the bishop and the priests were, as he supposed, equal as to the power of Orders, they were also equal as to the power of jurisdicition. Calvin differed from other Reformers who opposed all ecclesiastical authority as distinct from the universal priesthood of believers[54] in that he admitted a sacerdotal dignity in some, but defended its equality in all possessing that dignity, just as Aërius had done, and to the same practical effect. The Synod of Pistoia restricted its express claim to that of the equality of bishop and priests, especially pastors, *in synod.* Each of these claims was an historical innovation, as is apparent from the foregoing few but typical references, and a juridical error as will be evident from the following discussion.

II. Juridical Basis.

As to the question of law, there can be difficulty concerning the monarchic tenure of episcopal government only for those who in theory or in fact deny the divinely established hierarchical organization of the Church. The most radical opposition is found in the so-called democratic error which holds that the power of the Church was originally confided to the faithful in general and either *de facto* transferred or *de iure* to be transferred to the pastors, both bishops and priests, either directly or through the medium of the civil rulers, and consequently that the exercise of power is variously dependent on the acceptance of the people.[55] This claim, however, is against the hierarchy generically, and not specifically against the monarchic episcopate, which supposes a divinely instituted authoritative personnel distinct from the body of the faithful. The specific theory which claims the jurisdictional equality of priests and bishop is called that of

[54] I Pet., 2: 5, 9.

[55] This doctrine was first proposed by Marsilius of Padua (+ca. 1342) in the beginning of the fourteenth century, and adopted by many of the protestant sects in the sixteenth. It was condemned by John XXII in the constitution *"Licet,"* October 23, 1327,—*Fontes,* n. 38; cf. Zaccaria, *Storia Polemica delle Prohibizioni de'Libri* (Roma, 1777), pp. 93-122.

presbyteral aristocracy.[56] As advanced by Calvin and the other Reformers who recognized an essential distinction between clergy and laity, it was condemned in the council of Trent,[57] and as proposed by the Synod of Pistoia (1786) was proscribed by Pius VI in his constitution *"Auctorem Fidei"*, August 28, 1794.[58]

There are numerous variations in the theory of presbyteral aristocracy. All deny the radically independent nature of the bishop's position. Some admit a proper and principal jurisdiction to the bishop, but subject to the presbyteral right of participating deliberatively in the rule of the diocese. Others hold that pastors have *iure divino proper* power in their respective parishes over which the bishop's authority is extraordinary, to correct excess and supply defects in the pastors' regime.[59] Still others, and by far the greater number, contend that the bishop is superior in jurisdiction, but merely by consent of the priests, from whom the power derives, under whom it is exercised, and in whose name it is held.

The Code in Canon 334, 1, answers all of these errors and establishes beyond question the essentially independent nature of the residential bishop's position. It states that residential bishops are the ordinary and immediate pastors in the dioceses committed to them.[60]

[56] Cavagnis, *Institutiones Iuris Publici Ecclesiastici,* II, 449.

[57] "Si quis dixerit Episcopos non esse presbyteris superiores, vel non habere potestatem confirmandi et ordinandi, vel eam quam habent illis esse cum presbyteris communem . . . Anathema sit."—Sess. XXIII, c. 4, *de ordine,* canon 7—Mansi, XXXIII, 140.

[58] "Doctrinam, quae statuit, reformationem abusuum circa ecclesiasticam disciplinam in synodis dioecesanis ab episcopo et parochis aequaliter pendere ac stabiliri debere, ac sine libertate indebitam fore subjectionem suggestionibus et iussionibus episcoporum: falsa, temeraria, episcopalis auctoritatis laesiva, regiminis hierarchici subversiva, favens haeresi Aerianae a Calvino innovatae." —n. 19 (propositio nona damnata)—*Fontes,* n. 475.

[59] This particular aspect was advanced by the Jansenists who first applied it to the Pope as regards the diocesan bishops and then to the bishops' relation to the parochial affairs.

[60] "Episcopi residentiales sunt ordinarii et immediati pastores in dioecesibus sibi commissis."

The word *ordinary,* while it is ultimately referable to the power of the bishop, as used in the canon directly characterizes his person, which is being explicitly considered in this article. It signifies that his power is not entrusted to him personally but officially. It is not delegated, and he himself is not merely the delegate of any one within or without the Church, diocesan or extra-diocesan.[61] It further denotes that he holds his power, whatever it may be, for the usual, every-day conduct of the diocese, and not exclusively for extraordinary conditions or circumstances. Moreover, while it is not expressly stated, the title "ordinary" vindicated to the residential bishop in this canon equivalently characterizes the pastors of the dioceses. These latter have, by common law, ordinary power in the internal forum.[62] They are not ordinaries, however, in the sense by which the bishop is so called,[63] neither is the power or position which they possess held *iure divino.*

Just as there is no superior whom he merely represents as a delegate, so there is no divinly ordained inferior through whom the bishop must act.[64] He is the *immediate* pastor of the flock committed to his care.[65] This term indicates his relationship to other authorities in his diocese, and vindicates the native right of the bishop to exercise his authority independently of any other power, secular or clerical.[66] Lay interference always was and ever will be an abuse, whether it proceed from the faithful as

[61] Canon 197, § 1.

[62] Canon 873, § 1; 202, § 2.

[63] "Ordinarius simpliciter et absolute dicitur qui, ultra jurisdictionem ordinariam ad absolvendum, habet etiam ordinariam ad exercenda omnia alia munia spiritualia, etiam in foro exteriori."—Billuart, *Cursus Theologiae* (10 vols., Parisiis, 1904), IX, 356.

[64] "Episcopi in suis regendis dioecesibus nullo prorsus modo ex subditorum arbitrio pendent, neque ulli alii in agendis rebus quam Sedi Apostolicae rationem reddere debent."—Benedict XV, *Epistola ad Delegatum Apostolicum in Indiis Orientalibus,* 15 oct. 1921—*AAS,* XIV (1922), 7.

[65] Conc. Vat., Sess. IV, c. 3—Denzinger-Bannwart, *Enchiridion,* n. 1828.

[66] Pius IX, litt. encyc. *"Etsi multa,"* 21 nov. 1873—*Fontes,* n. 566; Leo XIII, ep. encyc. *"Immortale Dei,"* 1 nov. 1885—*Fontes,* n. 592; Pius X, litt. encyc. *"Iamdudum,"* 24 maii 1911—*Fontes,* n. 692.

such or from the civil authorities. As to clerics, the other diocesan officials required by the common law are of purely ecclesiastical origin and although both their position and their rights are sanctioned by that higher law, they are of their nature infra-episcopal and auxiliary, so that the bishop can in particular cases dispense with their help and officiate personally. He is as much the superior of the clerical,[67] as of the lay diocesans, in both their personal and their official aspects.

Aside from the historical basis of the monarchic episcopate, and the unique feature thereof as the only divinely instituted diocesan authority which supposes its endowment with all the necessary prerogative of complete and independent diocesan government, there is the reason for the monarchic tenure which arises from the same principle as the unitary system of episcopal government, namely, the unity of the Church, according to which the unity of the universal organization is reflected in each of its particular divisions.[68] Others who may have ordinary and immediate power in the external forum within the diocese, hold it in the name of their bishop; in order words, their power though ordinary is vicarious and subordinate. They are coadjutors of the bishop, or as in some extraordinary cases occurs, substitutes to the bishop, but in this latter instance with papal power and as the vicars of the Roman Pontiff.

Finally, it is usual to discuss in connection with the monarchic episcopate the question of how the individual bishop derives his authority. The apostles, as was seen above, chose their own fields of labor. Their successors as the canon states, are *assigned*

[67] Conc. Trid., Sess. XXIII, c. 4, canon 7—Mansi, XXXIII, 140; "Ecclesiae catholicae firmissimum dogma est, Episcopos esse superiores presbyteris, non solum ordinis potestate, sed etiam jurisdictionis."—Benedict XIV, *De Synodo Dioecesana*, lib. 13. c. 1, n. 2.

[68] "Accedit ratio unitatis Ecclesiae. Nam cum jurisdictio episcopalis participetur ab Ecclesia, quamvis ex voluntate Christi, cumque ad unitatem singulorum Ecclesiarum necessarium sit unus pastor, *ipsa rerum natura* fert illum qui praeeminet ordine, esse et jurisdictione investitum, secus si presbyteri essent ei pares, deficeret principium unitatis."—Cavagnis, *Institutiones Iuris Publici Ecclesiastici*, II, 525-526.

to a particular flock. As it is the prerogative of the Roman Pontiff alone to erect, divide, unite and suppress dioceses,[69] so it is his alone to appoint bishops over them. Others may by positive concession of the Church enjoy the privilege of electing, presenting or designating a candidate, but this of itself has merely a factual and not a juridical significance or consequence. Juridical status is born only of canonical mission,[70] the nomination by the Supreme Pontiff of the person as a participant in the apostolic office by the canonical provision of a diocese which he will govern.

Christ himself sent the apostles and gave them power for their official purpose. Both the purpose and the power were thereby once and for all created. The episcopal office and power in general cannot be altered; the episcopate cannot be either augmented or abridged by the Church as to its *ordinary potential* capacity. The individual bishop's office is a participation in that general office rather than a particularization thereof; his jurisdiction a participation in that general power rather than a particularization thereof. Both the office and the power exist prior to the bishop's participation in them, and are not substantially affected thereby.

The apostolic office is one, and the apostolic power inherent in that office is one. There can be no distinction between the apostolic office in one and the other diocese, since it is essentially one throughout the whole Church. There is also existentially but one episcopal office and power radically indivisable and consequently identical wherever found; there are, on the other hand, many officials. Each individual bishop holds and exercises the same office and power as all the others, without in the least detracting from the prerogatives of the others.[71] Individual epis-

[69] Canon 215, § 1.

[70] Conc. Trid., Sess. XXIII, c. 4, *de ordine*, canon 7—Mansi, XXIII, 138; canon 332 § 1.

[71] The variously interpreted expression of St. Cyprian: *"Episcopatus unus est, cuius a singulis in solidum pars tenetur"* (*De Catholicae Ecclesiae Unitate*, 5, 2—*MPL*, IV, 501) may best be understood in this sense. The unity of the Universal Church is reflected in each diocese, wherein a single bishop holds power essentially and substantially the same as that of all others, excepting that of the Bishop of Rome. The office and power of all bishops are both specifically and numerically identical.

copates are not actual particularizations of a generic authority, nor are they distinguished one from another by reason of distinct office and power. There is no division of episcopal power itself, but merely a duplication of persons who exercise it. The distinction between the general and the particular, as well as between the particulars themselves is one of officials and material object, the determination of which has been left by Christ to the judgment of the Church. The Church does not institute particular episcopates in the sense that she directly differentiates particular episcopal offices and powers, but merely in the sense that she appoints particular episcopal officials and apportions to each as the object of his office and power a particular episcopal object, a distinct territorial division of the Universal Church.

The Sovereign Pontiff, then, neither creates the particular purpose or determines the potential power of the bishop. He merely deputes the person of the bishop and assigns the latter a specific sphere of jurisdiction. The properly nominated person enters upon his office and acquires his power when he takes juridical possession of its material object, a particular territory, since episcopal jurisdiction is by its nature a territorial authority. Consequently, until the bishop acquires the possession of the object which he is to govern, he cannot validily function.[72]

When these notions are properly understood, there appears to be a possible solution of the question regarding the immediate source of the individual bishop's jurisdiction over his diocese beyond the alternatives of the celebrated controversy so agitated in the Council of Trent,[73] though left undecided and still freely disputed. The question was whether the individual bishop receives his jurisdiction immediately from God through episcopal consecration or rather immediately from the Sovereign Pontiff through canonical mission. Although the latter of these two alternatives is now the more commonly accepted, and although there are both historical and positive arguments for each view, it seems possible that the immediate derivation of the individual bishop's power,

[72] Canon 334 § 2.

[73] Cf. Lainez, *Disputationes Tridentinae* (2 vols., Oeniponte, 1886).

whether potential or actual, need not be traced in its authorship directly either to God or to His visible Vice-gerent in the Church.

It is obvious that Christ created the episcopal *office.* It is also obvious that to those whom He commissioned to that office He committed a *power* commensurate to it. It is also true, though possibly not always realized, that this power is really an entity distinct from the office, though necessarily consequent to and even concomitant with it. The words *"Going therefore, teach ye all nations,"* etc., even though they were pronounced in moral union with the words *"Whatsoever ye shall bind on earth,"* etc., nevertheless preceded the latter in the order of time and in the order of reason, and expressed respectively the assignment of the apostolic office and the confering of the apostolic powers upon those to whom they were spoken. The office itself was assigned before the power to fulfill it was confered. Though the office itself is a means to a higher end, namely, the purpose of the office, it is nevertheless a purpose or end in itself as related to the power of fulfilling it, since this power is the means to the fulfillment of the office. The power inheres in the office, but it exists there because of the office, and it follows in the real as in the rational order the existence of the office.

Christ, then, created the office and implanted the power in it. His Vicar, the Pope, who is the root and source of all holding of power in the Church, by consequence vests also the one who hold episcopal power; not indeed in the sense that he directly confers it, but in the sense that the Pope is deputed to designate the persons who are to be associated with himself in the government of the Church. It would seem, then, that as Christ incorporated the power into the office, so the Pope invests the person with the office, and that neither the One nor the other of them directly or immediately puts the person in power, but that both indirectly and mediately do so through the agency of the office. Whilst Christ and His Vicar must both be considered as embodying the source of episcopal power, Christ by the creation of the office together with its attendant power and the Pope by the designation of the incumbent and the assignment of a territorial object, yet it is only by a coalition of both these elements that the immediate source of jurisdiction is really provided.

The jurisdiction of the Sovereign Pontiff, full and complete, is in its character specifically distinct from that of the subordinate episcopate. The plenitude of the papal power, though sufficient for the complete and entire government of the Universal Church (so that in an *absolute* sense, and aside from the positive will of Christ, the separate power of other bishops might be said to be superabundant), and though more than equal to the power of the subordinate episcopate, does not essentially include the latter. Although the Pope possesses all the authority of the Church, he holds the jurisdiction of the lesser episcopate in the sense that he disposes of it, not as a share in his own, but as something radically different. The character of this jurisdiction is not the same as that of his own. The two powers are distinct species of ecclesiastical jurisdiction, and the Roman Pontiff, even considered merely as the bishop of the particular Roman diocese, exercises only one of them. It remains, then, in the consideration of the status of the subordinate episcopate, to examine the power thereof, both as constituted in itself and in relation to the jurisdiction of the Sovereign Pontiff.

Chapter III

THE POTENTIAL CAPABILITY

"Quas cum potestate ordinaria regunt sub auctoritate Romani Pontificis."

The third and final clause of canon 329 states that the bishops rule their respective dioceses with ordinary power but under the authority of the Roman Pontiff. This statement summarizes the potential capacity of episcopal power by indicating both its basic possibility and its radical limitations. The former is denoted by the description of the bishop's authority as ordinary. In the preceding chapter the fact of the bishop as the ordinary ruler of the diocese was discussed. The question here concerns the nature of the power which he wields as a consequence. The second concept involved in the notion of the potential capacity of the residential episcopate, its radical limitations, is expressed by the note of subordination with which the canon ends. This note of subordination must logically precede that of the ordinary specification. While the basic possibility ultimately depends on the radical limitations, the concept of these limitations is further dependent on the notion of the papal power. Consequently, the following discussion considers the episcopal power as the notion thereof is discernible from the essential characteristics of the papal primacy.

Article I
Subordinate Nature of the Diocesan Episcopate

This question must precede that of the basic nature of the bishop's ordinary power because the subordinate note of episcopal authority is a constitutive mark thereof. For while both the episcopal and the papal powers are of divine institution, their respective *notional* determination arises from an immediately different source. The supreme pontificate was altogether, both intensively and extensively, jurisdictionally determined by divine law in the fact of its institution.[1] The jurisdictional

[1] Solieri, *Institutiones Iuris Ecclesiastici*, p. 280.

potentiality of the subordinate episcopate was likewise *objectively* determined immediately and directly by the fact of its divine institution, although its *actual* realization was left to be determined by the Papal authority within certain limits according to circumstances. The concept of the papal power, however, is immediately and directly derived from the very fact of its establishment, whereas the *notion* of the episcopal potentiality must be deduced from the notion of the papal power, that is, by comparison with it, and by a coordinate process of elimination. Since the papal jurisdiction is the only higher authority in the Church, the nature of the lesser episcopate must be determined as implied therein, and the constitutive relation of the former to the latter is essentially a limitative one. It is not proposed to deal herein with the dogma of the Primacy as such, but only with regard to its juridical import in as far as this effects the intimate nature of the episcopate. The dogma as such has often and sufficiently been expounded. The question of its implicit determination of episcopal power may be considered as an historical fact and as a juridical feature.

I. Historical Relation of Papacy and Episcopate.

As has been said, the essential basis of episcopal jurisdiction, namely, the apostolic succession, was acknowledged both in theory and in practice from the beginning, and ultimately defined only in the Council of Trent against the Protestant innovations of the sixteenth century. Likewise, the unitary form and monarchic tenure have always been accepted existential features of the jurisdictional episcopate, though there are but few positive statements to be found in the law concerning it. The more directly canonical question, that is to say, the precise capacity or juridical extent of episcopal jurisdiction has a similar historical background. While the general notion of its nature has ever been uniform and in accordance with both the primitive practice and the ultimately required definitions, there is little to be found, until these latter were occasioned, in the way of explicit pronouncement on the matter, except what is equivalently contained in the various assertions of the Roman Primacy. This was, perhaps, natural in view of the intimate relation of the supreme and the subordinate episcopate.[2] When the balance is disturbed both are displaced. An attempt to weaken the papal power results in the increasing of the episcopal authority; and conversely, the undue advancement of episcopal authority must be an encroachment on the power of the Sovereign Pontiff.

In considering the relation of the two powers historically, one must clearly distinguish between the possession of a power and the exercise of the same. Thus, while Peter was as much the superior of the other apostles as the Sovereign Pontiff today is over the other bishops, nevertheless because of the universality and other unique prerogatives of the apostolic jurisdiction there was little occasion for the Prince of the Apostles to exercise his supreme power. Likewise, after the death of the apostles, during the time of the first propagation of the Church and its persecution, it was necessary to leave the maximum of possible autonomy to the single bishops in their respective dioceses. The central authority of the immmediate successors to St. Peter could not very well greatly influence the individual churches, burdened and encumbered as it was by both internal preoccupations arising from the circumstances attendant upon the early spread of the faith, and external impediments in the form of persecution.[3] When peace came for the Church, a greater organization both in members and on the part of authority appeared. By the year 150 the Roman Bishop came more to the fore as head of the universal Church, since the progress and development of events rendered a greater centralization not only possible but necessary. The many treatises which have appeared on the subject of the Primacy give numerous and conclusive historical examples of the Pope's accepted dominion over the whole Church, and his intervention in the affairs of individual dioceses, not only during this formative period but throughout the centuries as well. It is consequently unnecessary to repeat them here.

[2] ". . . Episcoporum potestas nec concipi per se nec salva consistere potest absque Summi Pontificis potestate."—Bachofen, *Summa Iuris Ecclesiastici Publici* (Romae: Pustet, 1910), p. 47.

[3] Cavagnis, *Institutiones Iuris Publici Ecclesiastici*, II, 403.

The question of the diocesan bishops' individual relation to the Pope first arose in the days of St. Cyprian, Bishop of Carthage, in the third century, and was not definitely settled until the Vatican Council in 1870. Meanwhile the Roman Primacy and its import regarding the residential bishops had been frequently asserted, though with few exceptions the matter at issue involved rather a point of practice than a point of principle. The rights of the Pope were in general recognized, but in their practical application there arose dissent as to their extent, and the final decree was required not so much to strengthen belief but to regulate behaviour.

Here again it is necessary to distinguish among the positive doctrines which attacked the essential basis of the papal position those which aimed at the social power of the Church in general and those which, though admitting a visible episcopal authority, specifically denied any superiority of one bishop over another as either of divine institution or of juridical necessity. Thus, the doctrine of Richer (1560-1631) proclaimed the radically democratic constitution of the Church and vindicated to the bishops in general only an instrumental and ministerial authority, and to the Pope a purely ministerial superiority over the other bishops, to be exercised exclusively in extraordinary instances. His book, "*De ecclesiastica et politica potestate,*" was several times condemned and prohibited.[4]

The specific error regarding the relation of the papal and diocesan episcopal authority is called that of *episcopal aristocracy.* It advances the equality of all bishops as to jurisdiction as well as to Orders, and was first set fourth by Photius and his followers in the Greek Schism of the ninth century. Admitting an historical primacy, they denied its divine right. Those of the Protestant sects in the sixteenth century which retained episcopacy claimed complete national autonomy, and it was largely in an effort to reconcile them to Roman Catholicism that several erroneous conceptions of the episcopal power were brought forth during the seventeenth and eighteenth centuries. While the theories here

[4] E.g., S. C. Indicis, 10 maii 1613; 2 dec. 1622.

mentioned directly were aimed at the Primacy, they resultantly affected the power of the individual bishop.

Gallicanism, which after a long process of brewing reached its quintessence in the famous "*Declaratio Cleri Gallicani*" (1681), did not deny the Primacy, but reduced it to one of inspection and direction only, and equivalently it increased the authority of the bishop in his diocese. On the strength of this doctrine the French bishops assumed more power over their sees, and Alexander VIII issued the Constitution "*Inter multiplices*"[5] condemning the Gallican tenets. The theories, however, spread from France, whence they had originated and where for a considerable time they had remained indigenous, and took root in the surrounding countries. In 1763 Febronianism, the German counterpart of Gallicanism, appeared. In his book entitled "*De statu Ecclesiae et legitima potestate Romani Pontificis,*" Febronius, under which name the author, Nicholas of Hontheim, auxiliary bishop of Treves, wrote, advanced to a radicalism far outstripping that of his Gallican teacher Van-Espen, though he merely carried Gallicanism to its logically inevitable conclusions. He held that on the strength of the Pseudo-Isidorian decretals the Popes from the ninth century onward had usurped many fundamental powers of the bishops, which should be restored to them, so that papal power would entail only those essential rights which it possessed during the first eight centuries. Febronius sought to increase the power of the bishops by assuring for them greater independence from the Pope; in actuality he succeeded in making them servilely subject to the civil power and the nationalist churches. His arguments have been answered from an historical aspect by Zaccaria.[6] Febronius' book was prohibited by Pope Clement XIII in 1764, but his doctrines reappeared in the writings of Eybel, which were likewise condemned by Pius VI in his Brief "*Super soliditate.*"[7] and in the propositions of the celebrated Synod of Pistoia (1786),

[5] 4 aug. 1690,—*Collectio Lacensis,* I, 831.
[6] Zaccaria, *Anti-Febronius* (2. ed., Louvain, 1829).
[7] 28 nov. 1786, —*Fontes,* n. 473.

the errors of which were condemned by the same Pontiff in his Constitution *"Auctorem fidei,"* referred to above.[8]

Thus, as distinguished from its correlative error, presbyteral aristocracy, which reduced the bishops to the status of the priests, the present doctrine, episcopal aristocracy, raised the bishops to a level with the Pope. The accumulation of all these errors finally occasioned the definition of the Vatican Council as to the exposition of the Church's nature and constitution and of the jurisdictional primacy of the Roman Pontiff, from which is clearly deducible the juridical status of the residential bishop, particularly as to the extent of his native potential authority. Theologians have adequately defended and scientifically proved the doctrine of the Primacy, the general import of which is evident, so that only the particular applications of the jurisdictional properties to the present topic are herein discussed.

II. Juridical Relation of Papacy and Episcopate.

The residential or subordinate episcopate's power is ordinary because it is inherent in the office,[9] and the purpose of the office occasions its specific possibilities. As has been stated, the bishop's authority is essentially jurisdictional. As resident in this particular office, however, the jurisdictional authority exists in the measure according to which it is modified by the limits of the office. The radical limitations of the episcopal office are both extrinsic and intrinsic.

1. Extrinsic Limitation.

The foregoing discussion concerning the unitary system of episcopal government discloses that one bishop only presides over a particular territorial division of the universal Church. The monarchic tenure of episcopal authority evidences the individual bishop's complete and independent control of the territory over which he presides, as opposed to any authority within the diocese. The bishop's authority is further immune to external

[8] 28 aug. 1794, —*Fontes,* n. 475.

[9] Canon 197, § 1: "Potestas jurisdictionis ordinaria ea est quae ipso iure adnexa est *officio* . . ." This applies whether the office be of divine or of purely ecclesiastical institution.

interference from any but papal authority; that is to say, each bishop is limited in the use of his power to the affairs of his own diocese. There has never been any real historical issue on this question, though there apparently were isolated instances of a contrary tendency which prompted the several positive statements which attest to the accepted traditional uniformity.[10]

The subordinate episcopate, then, is intended for the government of a diocese only, and the incumbent is invested with all the power that this implies. Its local extent determines the episcopal power as generically diocesan in its specific qualitative and quantitative object. Actually, however, it is not so extensive, since there are other limitations which intrinsically restrict its potential capacity.

2. Intrinsic Limitation.

The notion of episcopal ordinary power entails more than the abstract concept of ordinary power as potentially sufficient in itself for its end; for the government of a diocese has a unique relation to that of the whole Church. As Charles Augustine says of this ordinary power, "the term signifies a certain autonomy, but not complete independence." [11] While the bishop is in a certain sense supreme in his own church, the various churches themselves are not independent kingdoms. They are interrelated; and not because they unite synthetically to form the Universal Church, but because they are analytic units of a radically indivisible society,[12] under the unique hegemony of the Bishop of Rome, to whom each is bound in a way which must rather be described than defined. Consequently, the true concept of the

[10] Cf. Conc. Constantinop. (381), c. 2, quoted previously, —Mansi, III, 557; Pope Zosimus (417): "Omnes sane admonemus ut quisque finibus territoriisque suis contenti sint. . . ." —*Ep. I*, 3 —*MPL*, XX, 644; St. Bernard (1153): "Aliorum potestas certis arctatur limitibus, tua autem extenditur et in ipsos." —*De Consideratione*, ad Eugenium Papam II, 8 —*MPL*, CLXXXII, 752; St. Augustine (430): "Hoc est ridiculum dicere, quasi ad me pertineat cura propria, nisi Hipponensis ecclesiae. . . ." —*Ep. ad Eusebium*. —*MPL*, XXXIII, 133.

[11] *A Commentary on the New Code of Canon Law*, II, 172.

[12] Solieri, *Institutiones Iuris Ecclesiastici*, p. 273.

local bishop's ordinary power is impossible unless it includes the note of subordination, not merely as a characteristic which influences its practical exercise, but as an intrinsic determinant of its essentially potential capacity. Subordination is first of all a *qualitative* mark of the bishop's ordinary jurisdiction. For though the *ordinary* and the *subordinate* aspects of episcopal jurisdiction are separate attributes; they are so mutally affective that it is only by the fusion of their respective notional content that the potential capacity of the power which they existentially determine can be properly revealed. The power of the bishop is, indeed, ordinary, but the office is itself subordinate.

The subordinate nature of the episcopal office follows from the jurisdictional primacy of the Sovereign Pontiff as defined in the Vatican Council.[13] The ordinary jurisdiction which the Pope enjoys is explicitly described in the doctrinal definition by several attributes which equivalently indicate the status of all other jurisdictions in the Church, including even that only othei one which is of divine institution, the Episcopate. Primacy connotes exclusiveness. It is said to be *complete, supreme, universal* and *immediate.*[14] Each of these marks really implies the others,

[13] "Docemus proinde et declaramus, Ecclesiam Romanam, disponente Domino, super omnes alias ordinariae potestatis obtinere principatum, et hanc Romani Pontificis iurisdictionis potestatem, quae vere episcopalis est, immediatam esse: erga quam cuiuscunque ritus et dignitatis pastores atque fideles, tam seorsum singuli quam simul omnes, *officio hierarchicae subordinationis* veraeque oboedientiae obstringuntur, non solum in rebus, quae ad fidem et mores, sed etiam in iis, quae ad disciplinam et regimen Ecclesiae per totum orbem diffusae pertinent; ita ut, custodita cum Romano Pontifice tam communionis quam eiusdem fidei professionis unitate, Ecclesia Christi sit unus grex sub uno summo pastore. Haec est catholicae veritatis doctrina, a qua deviare salve fide atque salute nemo potest." —Sess. IV, c. 3 —Denzinger-Bannwart, *Enchiridion,* n. 1827.

[14] "Si quis itaque dixerit, Romanum Pontificem habere tantummodo officium inspectionis vel directionis, non autem *plenam* et *supreman* potestatem jurisdictionis in *universam* Ecclesiam, non solum in rebus, quae ad fidem et mores sed etiam in iis, quae ad disciplinam et regimen Ecclesiae per totum orbem diffusae pertinent; aut eum habere tantum potiores partes. non vero totam plenitudinem huius supremae potestatis; aut hanc eius potestatem non esse *ordinariam* et *immediatam* sive in omnes ac singulas

though since each is intended to answer a particular misconception, it expresses directly a special aspect of the papal power relative to other authorities. The plenitude and universality of the papal jurisdiction characterize the ordinary power of the residential bishop as fundamentally limited, whereas the supreme and immediate character of the former renders the latter functionally limitable. At this point only the fundamental limitations are considered, the functional limitability being relegated to the later discussion of the positive determination of episcopal authority. These are, then, the intrinsic limitations of episcopal jurisdiction as opposed to the extrinsic limitation of its local extent.

The *plenitude* of the papal power denotes chiefly that it alone is qualitatively all-intensive or complete, that is to say, that its potential capacity, and it alone, is equal to every social demand of the Church. This implies that the ordinary jurisdiction of the subordinate or residential bishop is insufficient for every need that qualifies as diocesan in the widest sense of the term. Its qualitative intensity is but partial. Its natural sufficiency does not embrace what is by nature only *relatively* diocesan. The doctrinal unity of the Church requires that the basic discipline of the Church be uniform, regardless of territorial distinctions, and necessitates a certain amount of common law which only the fullest possible competence can determine and impose. Consequently the theory advanced in the Synod of Pistoia to the effect that the bishop receives from Christ all rights necessary for the government of his diocese, and that therefore no higher and ulteriorly competent authority is required, was condemned.[15]

ecclesias sive in omnes et singulos pastores et fideles: anathema sit." —Sess. IV, c. 3 —Denzinger-Bannwart, *Enchiridion*, *n.* 1831.

[15] "Doctrina Synodi, qua profitetur, persuasum sibi esse, episcopum accepisse a Christo omnia jura necessaria pro bono regimine suae dioecesis: perinde ac si ad bonum regimen cuiusque dioecesis necessariae non sint superiores ordinationes spectantes sive ad fidem et mores, sive ad generalem disciplinam, quarum ius est penes summos Pontifices et Concilia generalia pro universa Ecclesia: schismatica, ad minus erronea." —Pius VI, Const. *"Auctorem fidei,"* 28 aug. 1794, n. 16 (propositio sexta damnata)—*Fontes*, n. 475.

The radically necessary common law, then, embraces matters for which the ordinary power of the residential bishop is essentially inadequate, precisely because they are only relatively diocesan in as far as they apply antecedently to and irrespective of any territorial division of the universal Church. Such matters are called the *essential causae maiores,* and include those which require infallibility of doctrine and which are contained in the dogmatic laws consequent to it,[16] as well as those purely disciplinary laws which concern the status of the universal Church.

The *universality* of the papal jurisdiction signifies primarily its exclusive qualitative extension, and further particularizes the potential capacity of the local bishop's ordinary power. The latter as exstrinsically limited is particularized as quantitatively territorial and as restricted by the *plenitude* of papal authority, would at most qualitatively comprehend whatever is *absolutely* diocesan, that is, whatever is diocesan in the generic sense that it is occasioned by and ordained to diocesan organization. However, ordinary episcopal power is not apt for even all that this implies. For there are many matters which, while occasioned consequent to diocesan organization, are not thereby *exclusively* diocesan. The reason is that, while they may be immediately conducive to the local needs, they are common to all dioceses as such. They are consequently of such universal import that uniformity, if not absolutely essential, is nonetheless eminently expedient and practically necessary. Such uniformity is possible only by papal ordinance.

A great portion of the common law is concerned with such affairs which constitute the so-called *causae maiores per se.* These comprehend especially those matters which pertain to the relation of the individual dioceses to the supreme authority of the Roman Pontiff or the relation of the several dioceses one to the other. These intrinsic limitations of the residential episcopate's ordinary jurisdiction, therefore, render the latter incompetent for all the major issues which are such either *essentially* or *per se.*[17]

[16] Cavagnis, *Instiutiones Iuris Publici Ecclesiastici,* II, 438-439.
[17] Cavagnis, *Institutiones Iuris Publici Ecclesiastici,* II, 438-439.

As will be seen in a later chapter, there are other *causae maiores* which are said to be so *per accidens,* in as much as they further delimitate the bishop's authority, not, however, as that authority is fundamentally subordinate, but rather as it is functionally dependent, since the bishop would be natively competent to manage them were they not *de facto* reserved to the Roman Pontiff by the positive law.[18]

Meanwhile, the immediate question to be considered is that of the basic possibility of the diocesan bishop's ordinary jurisdiction as that is deducible from the foregoing and correlative consideration of its radical limitations.

Article II

The Basic Possibility of the Subordinate Episcopate

Given the basic restrictions, both local and material, what is the *potential* range of the ordinary jurisdiction of the residential bishop? In view of the preceding comparison between the papal and the episcopal authority, it is evidently absurd to say, as some in the past have, that the bishop can do all within the limits of his diocese that the Sovereign Pontiff can do in the universal Church.[19] At the least, the creation of conflicting authorities within the diocese, each of equal competence, would be altogether inevitable from such a principle. At most, the practical abrogation of the papal authority would rather readily follow. The anterior principle of hierarchical subordination would be vitiated, if not entirely then certainly as far as any fundamental significance attaches to it, since the papal prerogative could at most, in such a case, extend to the exercise of a confirmatory or suggestive power. Moreover, the basic unity of the Church in both doctrine and discipline would be impossible, since each bishop could pronounce on all matters of belief and behavior as he saw fit.

On the other hand, in view of the purpose of his office such

[18] Canon 220.

[19] This tenet of Febronianism was condemned by Pius VI in his brief *"Super soliditate,"* 28 nov. 1786, n. 4 —*Fontes,* n. 473.

ample jurisdictional power must be basically vindicated to the bishop as is necessary for the good government of the diocese committed to him.[20] In doing so, however, account must be taken of the radical limitations which the nature of the Primacy imposes on the nature of the episcopacy. It must be remembered too in this regard that the positive statutes of the common law, which make up that part of it which is either essentially or practically necessary, merely contain and concern those major issues which are both *de iure* and *de facto* reserved to the supreme central authority of the Roman Pontiff. It must not, however, be concluded that these *de facto* reservations exhaust the possibility of *de iure* reservations. In other words, it does not necessarily follow that there are no others which, though not positively, are nevertheless naturally reserved, in that by their nature they require a supreme authority for their regulation. Consequently, it is not enough to say simply that in virtue of his ordinary power the diocesan bishop is *naturally* competent for all that is not *explicitly* reserved.[21]

Fagnanus, whom Benedict XIV cites in opposition to this view,[22] mentions several authors, e.g., Soto and Sanchez, as having held it. In order to disprove the proposition, specifically as to the bishop's dispensatory power, Fagnanus argues principally from the contention that the bishop's jurisdiction is immediately derived from the Pope rather than directly from God [23] and, although he reaches the proper conclusion as to the falsity of the statement, the basis of his proof does not seem to be pertinent, especially since its certainty is contested.

It is not the *origin* precisely, but rather the *purpose* of any authority which radically determines its potentiality. Thus, the statement at hand, to the effect that the bishop is as competent

[20] Ottaviani, *Institutiones Iuris Publici Ecclesiastici,* I, n. 220.

[21] " . . . ex eo dumtaxat quod aliquid non sit *expresse* Episcopis prohibitum, non licet inferre, idem esse eisdem positive concessum . . . " —Benedict XIV, *De Synodo Dioecesana,* lib. 9, c. 1, n. 7.

[22] Benedict XIV, *De Synodo Dioecesana,* lib. 9, c. 1, n. 5.

[23] Fagnanus, *Commentaria in Quinque Libros Decretalium* (4 vols., Venetiis, 1696), in cap. *Perniciosam, de officio ordinarii,* nn. 28-56.

in his diocese as is the Pope in the universal Church, excepting only that which is *explicitly* reserved, is false and untenable because it is insufficient, on the one hand, and curiously enough, too extensive on the other. First of all, it fails to consider the antecedent natural limitations which the relation of the papal and episcopal offices places on the latter's possibilities, that is, before and independent of any positive statute, and it reduces that relation to a purely practical one. On the other hand, it opens the way to the total abrogation of episcopal power, since the Pope might reserve everything and thus reduce the bishop's authority to naught.

It may, however, be said that the residential bishop's ordinary jurisdiction is competent *by nature* for all that is not *expressly*, that is, neither *explicitly* nor *implicitly* reserved or prohibited by the higher law.[24] By the latter is meant the divine positive law constitutive and definitive of the Church's constitution in general and of the papal Primacy in particular. The basic potentiality of episcopal jurisdiction, then, comprehends what is absolutely and exclusively, that is to say, *specifically* diocesan. That may be called absolutely and exclusively diocesan which, though occasioned by diocesan organization in the Church, is not thereby or *per se* common to all dioceses as such. It thus embraces the exigencies peculiar (though not necessarily unique) to the particular region comprised by the territorial limitations of the diocese, regardless of the fact that these needs exist habitually and regularly or that they arise only incidentally and circumstantially. That, considering the relation of the episcopal to the papal office, would seem to be the specifically intended purpose of the former in the Church as Christ disposed it. It must, however, be recalled that we are speaking here only of the *potential* possibilities of episcopal jurisdiction. For, as will be discussed later in regard to the function of that power, this basic possibility cay be, as it somewhat considerably is, further restricted in practice by the supreme and immediate qualities of the papal jurisdictional Primacy. It is in this sense that Suarez,

[24] Solieri, *Institutiones Iuris Ecclesiastici*, p. 280.

discussing the opinion whereby the bishop would be limited only by what is prohibited, says that while as it stands it is false, there is one sense in which it may be tenable if various limitations are sufficiently supposed.[25] That is to say, the axiom precisely as it stands claims too much regarding the episcopal authority, and may be accepted only if the bishop's competence is considered as both *relative* and *potential.* In other words, the bishop's purely potential competence is relatively as extensive in his diocese and relatively as potentially sufficient for its purpose as is that of the Roman Pontiff in the universal Church, since the potentially of both the papal and the episcopal authority are *naturally* restricted only by the higher law, the divine law constitutive of the Church.

Ordinary power is so called to distinguish it from delegated authority. It was seen above that the bishop's jurisdiction is not delegated to him by any authority within the diocese, whether priest or people. Neither is it delegated to him by the Roman Pontiff. In such a case the bishop's authority would be essentially papal. His office is not a delegated one, because it is not one through which the Pope governs a section ot the universal Church, but one by which the Church therein contained is specifically governed. There is a difference, and it is the difference between that which is merely auxiliary and that which is somewhat autonomous by native right, a norm which ecclesiastical history attests as a fact in the relation of bishop and pope. Arbitrary interference has never been customary from above, any more than it has been tolerated from below the bishop's authority.

[25] "Imprimis axioma, *Episcopus potest in suo episcopatu, quidquid Papa in Ecclesia, nisi prohibeatur,* et nullo jure fundatum est, et in rigore censeo esse falsum, nisi multis modis limitetur . . . Si in aliquo sensu id tolerari potest, solum est quoad ea quae pertinent ad ordinariam gubernationem moraliter necessariam vel convenientem ad salutem animarum, et considerando potestatem Episcoporum priusquam Pontifex aliquid agendum [i.e. positive] statuat vel prohibeat: sic enim intelligitur unusquisque Episcopus habere in tota sua dioecesi totam potestatem; quia *ex vi muneris conceditur,* et sic spectata non habet unde limitetur." —*Tractatus de Legibus,* lib. XI, cap. 14.

In his personal relations the bishop is as much the subject of the Sovereign Pontiff as any other Christian.[26] His official relation, however is unique, because his office is unique.

Ordinary power, as opposed to delegated authority, may be either proper or vicarious.[27] Episcopal jurisdiction is ordinary, not because it is annexed to the office of the bishop by the Church, but because it is implanted therein by Christ Himself. Since neither the office nor the power attached to it is the creation of the Church, but really that of Christ, both the office and the power are *held* only in his name,[28] regardless of how they are immediately acquired. In the visible hierarchy of the Church there is no one in whose stead the bishop governs, or assumes and carries out the government of his diocese. Consequently, it has always been the common teaching of theologians and canonists that the bishop's ordinary power is not merely vicarious but really proper to himself, in a word, that he acts in his own name.[29] Just as the bishop is not merely the delegate of any one in the Church, neither is he merely the vicar of the Pope in the ordinary conduct of his diocese.[30] It is consequently false to say that his authority is limited exclusively to those matters for which he is expressly commissioned by the Roman Pontiff. Although it may not have been his intent, the words of Fagnanus seem susceptible of this interpretation, namely that since the bishop's jurisdiction is obtained directly from the

[26] "Episcopi non solum non sunt Pontificis pares, sed ita eius auctoritati subduntur, ut, qui pastores appellantur et sunt, si populos respicias, ii, si Pontificem spectes, nonnisi ovium numero habeantur."—Pius VI, *Responsio super Nunciaturis* (Florentiae, 1790), p. 231.

[27] Canon 197, § 1.

[28] Hence St. Ignatius of Antioch writes: "It is manifest, therefore, that the Bishop should be regarded as the Lord Himself." —*Eph.* VI, 1 —Lightfoot, *The Apostolic Fathers*, II, 46.

[29] Bouix, *Tractatus de Episcopo*, I, 104.

[30] Quamquam vero neque plenam neque universalem ii, neque summam obtinent auctoritatem, non tamen *vicarii* romanorum pontificum putandi, quia potestatem gerunt sibi *propriam*, verissimeque populorum, quos regunt, antistites *ordinarii* dicuntur." —Leo XIII, ep. encycl. *"Satis cognitum,"* 29 iun. 1896, n. 25 —*Fontes*, n. 630.

Pope, it extends only to those things which the Sovereign Pontiff has designated.[31] Such a limitation would naturally follow from his status as merely a vicar of the Pope; it is, however, a limitation which was never, either on principle or in practice, even remotely claimed by the one or recognized by the other.

Since all ordinary power in reference to its scope receives a broad and liberal interpretation,[32] so that any objective doubt concerning its exclusive limits will not prohibit its optional use,[33] a *proper* ordinary will, therefore, under like circumstances of doubt always posit a presumption for its use both validly and licitly, unless and until it can be definitely proved that a contrary regulation obtains in a given case. For in every official there resides, besides his clearly marked power, a certain discretionary power in all that touches on his office. Proper ordinary authority, therefore, entails in its exercise a discretinary competence and a personal latitude beyond that which is enjoyed by him who acts for another as his vicar. As the proper ordinary of the diocese, the residential bishop is said to have in his favor an intention founded in law, that is to say, his authority presumably extends to all that does not require delegated or vicarious papal power and which is not opposed to the common law.[34] On this principle, those who contest the bishop's prerogative in any given case, must prove their contention by citing the law, for if the law is silent on the matter at issue, the presumption is in the bishop's favor, until the higher authority speaks.[35]

31 " . . . deducitur falsitas propositae assertionis, quod Episcopi circumscriptis reservationibus Apostolicis possint in suis dioecesibus quidquid potest Papa in Ecclesia universali: nam si potestatem jurisdictionis recipiunt Episcopi immediate a Papa, . . . necessario hinc sequitur, ut illam dumtaxat habeant partem jurisdictionis, ad quam secundum Canonicas sanctiones sunt vocati ab Ecclesia Romana."—*Commentaria, loc. cit.*, n. 54.

32 Canon 200, §1.

33 Augustine, *A Commentary on the New Code of Canon Law,* II, 178.

34 Ottaviani, *Institutiones Iuris Publici Ecclesiastici,* I, n. 220.

35 "Rem itaque integram et in sua potestate positam aggrediens Episcopus, libertate sua utatur oportet; ubi jura silent, loco legis est Praesulis auctoritas, praesertim vero quod, ut Doctorum fert adagium, Episcopus *intentionem habet in jure fundatam* in rebus omnibus quae ad dioecesim suam adminis-

Thus far, the episcopate has been examined as to its juridical status or official potentiality. The residential bishop is the monarchic successor to the ordinary apostolic authority and as such has potentially all specifically diocesan jurisdiction. The actual significance of this power appears in its use both as naturally and positively determined. The juridical function of the episcopate, therefore, remains to be considered.

trandam attinet." —Leo XIII, Const. "*Romanos Pontifices,*" 8 maii 1881, n. 16 —*Fontes*, n. 582.

PART TWO

THE JURIDICAL FUNCTION OF THE EPISCOPATE

"Ius ipsis et officium est gubernandi dioecesim tum in spiritualibus tum in temporalibus cum potestate legislativa, iudiciaria, coactiva ad normam sacrorum canonum exercenda,"

—CANON 335.

PRELIMINARY REMARKS

The term *juridical function,* as previously explained, is the correlative of the term *juridical status.* In its broadest sense it denotes the entire authoritative activity of the perfect society. Practically, since all authority is of necessity invested in individual members of the society, the term juridical function signifies the socially authorized exercise of a particular social office, the actual performance of a particular social commission. It may best be defined as the *potential capability* of the authority in question as determined in practice.

Juridical function, therefore, follows upon juridical status, since action must correspond to ability. It is, then, the logical as well as the ontological consequent of juridical status. Authority is ordained to action, and no power is *actual* until it is exercised and only while it is in use. As distinguished, therefore, from juridical status or *potential* capability, the real but merely *possible* scope of authority, juridical function is a real in the sense of an *actual* entity.

Moreover, just as the juridical status of any particular social authority is determined by the intrinsic factor of its specific purpose, so the juridical function of the same authority is dependent upon external influences. Authority is actively influenced both as to its use and as to its efficacy by extrinsic factors which either respond to or restrict its native capability. Thus, the subordinate episcopate discussed above in regard to its juridical status is *potentially* capable of all jurisdictional matters which are specifically diocesan by their nature. It is, however, actively restricted by the papal prerogative of immediately regulating many such matters. Thus, the subordinate episcopate may be curtailed as to its *objective comprehension* by the partial or entire withdrawal of otherwise diocesan matters from its actual jurisdiction; or it may be determined as to its *operative competence* by superior regulations prohibiting or prescribing certain methods of procedure. The concept of juridical function, therefore, is derived from an analysis of the juridical status with a particular view to its *objective comprehension* and *its operative competence,* and such a concept results in nothing other than a notion of the *actual capacity* of the authority investigated.

As for the foregoing estimate of the status, so for the present correlative exposition of the function of the episcopate, the Code of Canon Law provides a vehicle which in substance is sufficient and in form equally satisfactory. The general declaration of canon 335, however, which summarizes the juridical function of the residential episcopate, is more explicitly of juridical significance than the former canon. Though it does not immediately follow the former canon, it is none the less the proximate conclusion of canon 329, and furthermore, it more immediately bespeaks the several problems embraced.

This second section is, therefore, properly based on the statement of canon 335, and will adopt the evident division thereof. It deals in three chapters with *the operative competence, objective comprehension* and the *actual capacity* of the episcopate respectively. While the generic import of this canon is all-inclusive, embracing as it does the whole sphere of episcopal government, so that a commentary thereon might possibly involve detailed reference to the numerous particulars embodied in the entire range of canonical legislation pertinent to the episcopal power, the specific purpose of the proposition is to establish beyond doubt the basic prerogatives of the residential bishop's jurisdictional activity. These latter, then, are the pertinent aspects of the above-mentioned chapter headings, and are severally presented in the articles included under the same.

Chapter IV

THE OPERATIVE COMPETENCE

"Ius ipsis et officium est gubernandi dioecesim"

The first clause of canon 335 states that it is both the right and the duty of the residential bishop to *govern* his *diocese.* This proposition expresses the operative competence of episcopal jurisdiction as demanded by its essence and determined by its potential capability. This capability was said in the foregoing section to extend to all that is absolutely and exclusively, or in other words, *specifically diocesan.* As was also pointed out, a diocese is but a part of the universal Church and so has a particular relation thereto, in as much as it is not completely autonomous. Consequently, although a certain fundamental competence must be vindicated to the diocesan bishop, not only in theory but in practice as well, in virtue of his divinely established status, this prerogative must be tempered in view of the general purpose of the Church. Episcopal power is not only fundamentally limited in its potential capability, but is also functionally determinable according to the exigencies of the Universal Church. The following discussion will, therefore, treat of these two aspects in separate articles dealing respectively with the generic scope of the bishop's office in view of its apostolic essence, and the specific scope of that office determined within its potentiality in virtue of the higher papal authority.

Article I

Generic Scope of Episcopal Authority

To govern means, as St. Thomas Aquinas says,[1] to lead or to direct that which is governed to its proper end by apt means. This entails an authoritative competence of direction commensurate with the importance and perfection of the end. The end of a diocese is essentially the same as that of the Church in

[1] "Gubernare est, quid quod gubernatur, convenienter ad debitum finem perducere.—*De Regimine Principum,* I, c. 14.

general. That end is not specifically differentiated, nor is it numerically isolated by diocesan boundaries within the Church. The purpose of a diocese is ultimately the salvation of souls. For this purpose the same means must be employed within the diocese as are used by the Church at large, namely, the teaching of Christian truth and the governing of the faithful according to that doctrine. The bishop, therefore, in his jurisdictional capacity must be empowered to execute both these functions, he must be both the teacher and the ruler of his diocese.

I. Doctrinal Office.

Canon 1326 of the Code of Canon Law sets forth succinctly and sufficiently the magisterial commission confided to the bishop in virtue of his position as ruler over the souls committed to him. It states that, although bishops singly do not enjoy infallibility in teaching, they are nevertheless under the authority of the Roman Pontiff truly doctors and instructors of the faithful within their diocese.[2]

The bishop is the one authentic and divinely appointed teacher of faith and morals with his diocese.[3] The bishop, in virtue of his jurisdiction, is obliged to teach the Catholic faith within his own district,[4] and does so *authoritatively*. In general, the power of authoritative teaching implies complete jurisdiction over the domain of doctrine. It has, however, various degrees. "Simple bishops, placed over only a portion of the Christian flock,

[2] "Episcopi quoque, licet singuli vel etiam in Conciliis particularibus congregati infallibilitate docendi non polleant, fidelium tamen suis curis commissorum, sub auctoritate Romani Pontificis, veri doctores seu magistri sunt."

[3] "Ille dicitur in Ecclesia magister seu doctor authenticus, qui, ex officio divinitus instituto ius et obligationem pariter habet custodiendi, praedicandi ac propagandi doctrinam revelatam, atque, ex eadem divina ordinatione, ius habet exigendi fidem doctrinae a se traditae." —Hervé, *Manuale Theologiae Dogmaticae* (5. ed., 4 vols., Parisiis: Berche et Pagis, 1929), I, n. 461.

[4] "Quoniam igitur fides est ad salutem necessaria, omnino praedicari verbum Christi consequitur oportere. Profecto praedicandi hoc est docendi, munus *iure divino* penes magistros est, quos *Spiritus Sanctus posuit Episcopos regere Ecclesiam Dei.*" —Leo XIII, ep. encycl. "*Sapientiae christianae,*" 10 ian. 1890, n. 8—*Fontes*, n. 605; canon 1327, § 1.

possess only a partial and subordinate, and hence an imperfect and dependent, Power of Teaching. The Chief of the Episcopate, as Pastor of the entire flock, alone possesses the universal, sovereign, and hence complete and independent, Power of Teaching, to which the Bishops themselves must submit. The difference between his power and theirs appears most strikingly in the legal force of their respective doctrinal decisions,"[5] as will be seen later when the actual functional intensity of the residential bishop's jurisdiction is discussed.

The bishop alone is the successor to the apostles. He, and he alone, has received the apostolic commission. There may be others in his diocese, who are abler, of greater intellectual gifts, more brilliant, more profound, more eloquent, more widely read theologians, more commanding personalities, better fitter to expound the truths of revelations, but it is from him that these latter receive their power to teach and in whose office they participate. It was precisely in order that they might the better exercise this right and fulfill this duty of teaching which they considered their prime concern that the apostles were first prompted to commit to others, namely deacons, a share in their other apostolic labors.[6] It is the bishop who is the divinely appointed public teacher of his people. Others in his diocese can only teach publicly at all, in so far as he permits, or calls them to assist him in his labors.[7]

Thus the proposition of the Synod of Pistoia which proclaimed that pastors and other priests in diocesan synod assembled were along with the bishop true judges in matters of faith by reason of their ordination was condemned by Pius VI.[8]

[5] Wilhelm-Scannell, *A Manual of Catholic Theology* (4. ed., 2 vols., London, 1909), I, 34-35.

[6] Acts 6:2-4; "Officium docendi commisit Christus Apostolis, quorum vicem gerunt Episcopi, ut ipsi illud exercerent tanquam principalissimum . . . Officium autem baptizandi commisit Apostolis ut per alios exercendum, et hoc ideo quia in baptizando nihil operatur meritum et sapientia ministri sicut in docendo"—St. Thomas Aquinas, *Summa Theologica,* p. 3ª, q. 67, a. 2; cfr. II Tim. 1:2.

[7] Canon 1327, § 2.

[8] "Item doctrina, qua parochi aliive sacerdotes in Synodo congregati pro-

The bishop as teacher is constituted the promoter, the guardian and the vindicator of Christian doctrine in his diocese, and consequently has the right of inquiring into all whatsoever pertains to the conservation, defense and propagation of the faith therein.[9] He has the right by word, writing or work, personally or through others to teach sacred doctrine, according to whatever means he prefers.[10] Thus also, the bishop may in certain circumstances forbid others to teach publicly during the time in which he personally exercises his doctrinal office.[11]

The bishop's authoritative teaching commands the assent of all his subjects. They cannot reject it or pass it by because they think they know better. They must remember that God has appointed him their guide in faith and morals. Although it is quite possible that the individual bishop may err in what he teaches, since he is not personally infallible, the mere possibility of error in a teacher exempts no one from the duty of believing. In the rare contingency that the bishop should teach something which an individual subject may know to be at variance with the admitted doctrines of the Church, or if there are serious reasons for questioning his statements, assent may, or in the former instance, must be withheld. However, in the ordinary circumstances of life, and where no grave reason for doubt presents itself, the refusal to believe the bishop's teaching in matters of faith and morals is to reject a message which purports to

nuntiantur una cum episcopo judices fidei, et simul innuitur, judicium in causis fidei ipsis competere iure proprio, et quidem etiam per ordinationem accepto: falsa, temeraria, ordinis hierarchici subversiva, detrahens firmitati definitionum judiciorumve dogmaticorum Ecclesiae, ad minus erronea." —Const. *"Auctorem fidei,"* 28 aug. 1794, n. 18 (propositio decima damnata) —*Fontes,* n. 475.

[9] Deshayes, *Memento Iuris Ecclesastici* (Parisiis, 1895), n. 635.

[10] "Ius habet episcopus, quo modo sibi libuerit, verbo, scripto et opere, per seipsum aut per alios sacram doctrinam docendi." —Deshayes, *Memento Iuris Ecclesiastici,* n. 636.

[11] Canon 1343, § 2: "Et recte quidem; etenim quum solus Episcopus in sua dioecesi sit publicus Doctor et Magister, indecens profecto est ut, eo docente, quisquam discipulorum docere praesumat."—Benedict XIV, *De Synodo Dioecesana,* lib. 9, c. 17, n. 6.

be divine, conveyed by a messenger known to be divinely appointed. The way is thereby opened for the Protestant practice of private judgment. The bishop in his teaching capacity represents the apostles. Hence, his religious teaching has a claim upon his flock, which no other teaching, except the infallible teaching of the Church, can possibly have.

The teaching power of the bishop is summarily expressed by St. Thomas Aquinas, who says that the instruction of the faithful concerning the profound mysteries of faith and the perfection of Christian life pertains officially to the bishop.[12] We speak here merely of the prerogative itself and not of the scope or variously specified functional force thereof, which pertains to the discussion of the objective comprehension and actual capacity of the bishop's jurisdiction activity. Meanwhile, the power of the bishop to rule his diocese in accordance with Christian truth and within the limits of his official authority remains to be examined.

II. Disciplinary Office.

The government of a diocese involves not only the presentation with an authoritative voice of Catholic doctrine and principle, but also the equally authoritative direction and guidance of the faithful according to doctrinal truth and in the application of its principles to the conduct of their daily lives. The residential bishop can and must supervise the practice of faith within his diocese. Although the doctrinal basis itself of Christian life must be uniform throughout the Church universal, and although the general practice which that truth demands must also be one and the same wherever the faith is professed, a society so widely diffused as the Church will inevitably have needs peculiar to its particular localities. The larger the social body is, the more widely it extends, the more need will there be to provide for local conditions and necessities. One single code will not be similarly applicable in all its details to every portion of the

[12] " . . . instructio de profundis mysteriis fidei et perfectione vitae christianae . . . ex officio pertinet ad episcopos."—*Summa Theologica,* p. 3a, q. 71, a. 4 ad tertium.

Christian flock in the practice of the Christian faith. There must be local provisions to provide for this variety of local differences.

In this regard each bishop in his diocese, and under certain well-defined limitations is to his flock what the Soverign Pontiff is to the universal Church.[13] Within these well-defined limitations the authority of the Church is in his hands to exercise.[14] In virtue of the potential capacity of the authority inherent in the office which he holds, the bishop is not merely the nominal head of the diocese but the real soverign over it.[15] He is the radical source of all other diocesan authority. He disposes concerning the participation of others in the ecclesiastical authority of the diocese and directs authoritatively its use.[16]

Before discussing the limitations of this prerogative a word is necessary concerning the obligatory force of the residential

13 "Sicut Romanus Pontifex totius est Ecclesiae magister et princeps, ita Episcopi rectores et capita sunt Ecclesiarum quas rite singuli ad gerendum acceperunt." —Leo XIII, ep. encycl. *"Cum multa,"* 8 dec. 1882, n. 4 —*Fontes,* n. 587.

14 "Participes enim sunt sacrae potestatis, quam Christus Dominus a Patre acceptam Ecclesiae suae reliquit." —Leo XIII, ep. encycl. *"Cum multa,"* 8 dec. 1882, n. 4 —*Fontes,* n. 587.

15 "Christianae rei administratio, proxime et secundum Pontificem Romanum ad episcopos pertinet, qui scilicet quanquam pontificalis fastigium potestatis non attingunt, sunt tamen in ecclesiastica hierarchia *veri principes,* cumque singulas ecclesias singuli administrent, sunt *quasi prinicipales artifices in aedificio spirituali."* —Leo XIII, ep. encycl. *"Sapientiae christianae,"* 10 ian. 1890, n. 19 —*Fontes,* n. 605.

16 "In aedificio autem spirituali sunt quasi manuales operarii, qui particulariter insistunt curae animarum, puta sacramenta ministrando, vel aliquod huiusmodi particulariter agendi; sed quasi principales artifices sunt Episcopi, qui imperant, et disponunt qualiter praedicti suum officium exsequi debeant; propter quod et Episcopi, id est superintendentes, dicuntur." —St. Thomas Aquinas, *Quodlibet.,* I, q. vii, a. xiv.

"Solus episcopus proprie praelatus ecclesiae dicitur, et ideo ipse solus quasi sponsus annulum ecclesiae recipit, et ideo solus ipse habet plenam potestatem in dispensatione sacramentorum et jurisdictionem in foro causarum quasi persona publica. Alii autem secundum quod ab eo eis committitur." —St. Thomas, *Comm. in IV Sent.,* (ed. Vives, Parisiis, 1873), dist. XX, q. I, a. IV, q. 4.

bishop's authority. His potential capacity to regulate authoritatively whatever qualifies as specifically diocesan is beyond cavil. The recognition of this principle must be the determinant of obedience to his authority. The authority of the bishop regards not only principles but their concrete application, and he is not only the one divinely appointed teacher of doctrine, but also the one divinely ordained ruler of conduct and regulator of discipline. He is empowered not only to decide and judge of right and wrong principles of truth, but also to determine the application of these truths to practical life, and his authority has the same claim on the obedience of his subjects in one capacity as in the other.

It is true that by positive law the potential capacity of episcopal jurisdiction is determined and limited in many and various ways. It is true that in the use of his actual authority the individual bishop may excede the legitimate extent not only of his actual but of his potential power as well. However, because in the ordinary circumstances of his regime the bishop will but rarely at most go beyond his capacity either potential or actual, the acceptance of his disciplinary dispositions must be the practical reaction of all those who fall under his jurisdiction, notwithstanding their own views on the merits of the case in question. His disciplinary authority is no more infallible than is his teaching of doctrinal issues, but in the former as in the latter the public good and welfare demand that his authority be reverently esteemed and sustained. The measure of obedience due to it is not the degree of its infallibility. Neither is it the measure of suitability, opportuneness or effectuality in the minds of individual subjects.

The bishop's disciplinary authority is, of course, not absolutely final, since it is not, as is said, wholly *sui iuris*.[17] However, though appeal or recourse from it is admissible, it is recognized that the procedure thereto must be such as to preserve the re-

[17] "Romani pontificis potestas summa est, universalis, planeque sui iuris, episcoporum vero certis circumscripta finibus, *nec plane sui iuris.*"—Leo XIII, ep. encycl. *"Satis cognitum,"* 29 iun. 1896, n. 31 —*Fontes,* n. 630.

spect due to the episcopal authority and the general order of the diocesan organization.[18] Consequently, the intrinsic efficacy and force of episcopal jurisdiction is well evidenced in the fact that the reference of matters to the higher authority is generally not suspensive of the bishop's decision, so that most frequently until an appeal is taken and allowed or until the recourse which was had results in the bishop's action being overruled, his decisions stand and bind in conscience.[19] The principle is an important one, and, as is readily evident, without its recognition and acceptance all episcopal jurisdiction could be reduced to naught, and would be practically valueless as an actual factor in diocesan government.[20]

Article II

Specific Scope of Episcopal Authority

Thus far the ordinary authority of the residential bishop has been discussed in regard to its fundamental or intrinsic limitations as they are determined from a relative comparison with the exclusive papal prerogatives, as well as the basic extent of the episcopal power as deduced therefrom, in other words, its potential capability and function. As a subordinate species of ecclesiastical jurisdiction, however, the episcopal power of

[18] "Ut summum, in gravi aliqua conquerendi materia [contra episcopum], concessum est rem totam ad Pontificem Romanum deferre; id tamen *caute moderateque,* quemadmodum studium suadet communis boni, non clamitando aut objurando, quibus modis dissidia verius offensionesque gignuntur, aut certe augentur." —Leo XIII, ep. *ad Archiep. Turonen.,* 17 dec. 1888—*ASS,* XXI (1889), 321.

[19] Cf., e.g., canons 192, § 3, 1340, § 3, 1395, §2, 1428, § 3, 2243, §1. "In dubio facti, quod non reincidit in dubium iuris, quando res pertinet ad genus in quo constat Superiorem posse praecipere, subditi tenentur obedire, si res probabiliter non excedit competentiam Superioris, salvo recursu ad Sanctam Sedem." —Van Hove, *De Legibus Ecclesiasticis* (Dessain: Mechliniae, 1930), n. 86.

[20] "Ex quibus apparet, adhibendam esse adversus episcopos reverentiam praestantiae muneris consentaneam in iisque rebus quae ipsorum potestatis sunt, obtemperari opportere." —Leo XIII, ep. encycl. *"Cum multa sint,"* 8 dec. 1882, n. 4 —*Fontes,* n. 587.

government is functionally determined, that is, in the actualization of its native potentiality, by positive juridic act rather than by its purely potential aptitude. Its actuality is not necessarily equal to its fullest possibility, although it may be so. Consequently, the complete concept of the bishop's actual prerogatives involves a notion of this functional determination, which itself further characterizes the actual scope and capacity of episcopal jurisdiction. In this matter there is necessary the separate consideration of the juridical fact itself and of the factors according to which the fact may be evidenced in the practical relation of the papal and the episcopal authority.

I. Natural Dependence.

By its very nature as divinely instituted the episcopal authority is subordinate and subject to the papal authority. This subordination and subjection must be understood not only in the sense that it is inferior as to its potentiality but also in the sense that its actual competence may be, and in many instances must be, concretely determined by the higher authority.[21] This does not imply, as was stated previously, that the bishop is competent only for those things which are expressly permitted him by the Pope, since this would render him both practically and in principle the vicar of the Pope and nothing more. On the contrary, it merely signifies that though the bishop's *potential* capability may be determined by its fundamental relationship to the primatial jurisdiction of the Roman Pontiff its *actual* capacity within those natural bounds was left by Christ to be more or less determined by the supreme authority of the Pope as times and circumstances, either universal or local, demand.[22]

[21] "Inferioris ordinis Episcopatus, eo ipso quod ex divina institutione *superiori auctoritati fuerit obnoxius,* ab hac suam *in concreto determinationem recipit,* ideo ut illa *pascendi vel regendi* auctoritas iure divino ad Episcopos, Apostolorum in ordinaria potestate successores, transmittatur, attamen ab Ecclesiastica suprema auctoritate ad ordinarium regimen *determinanda.*" —Solieri, *Institutiones Iuris Ecclesiastici,* p. 278.

[22] "Quoad episcopos, cum ipsorum gradus habeat potestatem subordinatam Pontifici, et limitatam [i.e. quoad *potentiam radicalem*], sed iure divino determinata non sit eiusdem intensitas [i.e. *actualis*], sequitur ipsorum

This dependence of episcopal jurisdiction on the actual determination of the Sovereign Pontiff must not be conceived as either *absolute* or *arbitrary*. The episcopate as well as the papacy was instituted by Christ for a definite purpose. This purpose is, therefore, of divine origin and is consequently immutable. The power ordained to this purpose must as a result remain substantially unchanged.[23]

The dependence of episcopal jurisdiction in its actual capacity on the positive determination of the Pope is not absolute, either in the sense explained above whereby the bishop would be competent only for what is expressly permitted him, or in the sense that his native potentiality may be so limited or restricted in scope or intensity as to render the bishop merely a nominal authority.[24] Although by the fact of its divine institution the ordinary and immediate power of the individual residential bishop, unlike that of the Pope, is not actually determined as to that which is to constitute its territorial or personal object, and although the same authority is only generally determined as to particular acts and matters, the fact of its institution nevertheless demands that the potential capacity of episcopal jurisdiction be left *substantially perfect* in its actual use.[25] The precise

positionem juridicam determinari iure ecclesiastico . . . Igitur pro temporum et locorum circumstantiis poterit Summus Pontifex ipsorum auctoritatem ampliare vel restringere . . ." —Cavagnis, *Institutiones Iuris Publici Ecclesiastici,* II, 474.

23 "Christus instituit primatum immediate, at non minus immediate instituit episcopatum, tum quoad ordinem sacrum cum quoad jurisdictionem, sed tamen ita ut, Episcopi, juxta ipsius Fundatoris voluntatem jurisdictionem nonnisi dependenter a Primatu exercerent actu remanerentque subjecti Romano Pontifici, qui tamen *non arbitrario modo,* sed juxta temporum locorumque rationem *et salva remanente verae ordinariaeque jurisdictionis substantia* disponere poterit ex plenitudine potestatis de extensione et intensione jurisdictionis singulorum Episcoporum." —Bachofen, *Summa Iuris Ecclesiastici Publici,* p. 25.

24 "Etsi autem intensitas potestatis ipsorum non sit definita, sed plus vel minus limitabilis pro temporum opportunitate, non ita limitari potest ut illusoria reddatur Christ institutio, adeo ut nomine tenus sint principes et non re"—Cavagnis, *Institutiones Iuris Publici Ecclesiastici,* II, 453.

25 "At maxima existit differentia inter potestatem iurisdictionis R. Pon-

meaning of this perfection will be seen from the discussion of the bishop's actual capacity in the government of his diocese. The episcopal power is substantially perfect when it entails the twofold faculty, doctrinal and disciplinary, which is necessarily involved in complete ecclesiastical jurisdiction. The substantial faculties need not be possessed of the fullest possible scope or intensity. They must, however, be capable of some truly doctrinal and disciplinary force, sufficient, that is, to allow all the external manifestations of complete jurisdictional activity. It must be remembered here, however, that it is not the actual authority of any and every individual bishop which is so characterized, but rather the power of the subordinate episcopate in general. The episcopate is an essentially necessary feature of practical ecclesiastical government by divine disposition. As such it is necessarily inclusive of a certain number of individual residential bishops. The exact number which would satisfy this requirement is not defined, though it would seem that a reasonable plurality is indicated. As long as the substantial authority of such a plurality is allowed, the jurisdiction of any particular bishop may be in its actual determination entirely at the disposal of the Pope. It is the jurisdiction of the necessarily existent bishops with which we are concerned. There are, in other words, some bishops who must as distinct from the Pope be real rulers within their diocese, whose native potentiality must not be so restricted in actual practice as to preclude the possibility of

tificis et Episcoporum: ille enim, vi institutionis Christi, certam et immutabilem potestatem obtinet, cui omnes fideles et omnia negotia spiritualia directe (alia negotia indirecte, pro necessitate finis spiritualis) subiiciuntur: Episcoporum jurisdictio hoc tantum sensu institutionis est divinae, quod communi modo Pontifex episcopos in partem sollicitudinis suae adhibere debeat, ad regendum sub se Ecclesiam cum potestate *ordinaria, immediata, perfecta* etiam quoad forum externum. At talis potestas iure divino determinata non est quoad *personas* tales vel tale *territorium,* nec etiam nisi *generatim* circa actus et materias: R. Pontifex eam amplificare aut restringere potest, dummodo maneat potestas *substantialiter* perfecta etiam in foro externo (legisfera, judiciaria, coactiva)." —Rivet, *Institutiones Iuris Ecclesiastici Privati* p. 371.

its substantially perfect actualization,[26] and render it almost useless or at least superfluous for the government of the Church.[27]

If the authority of the bishop were absolutely and entirely dependent in the sense that there were no ordinary capacity or power of the government inherent in the episcopal office and that consequently the bishop were competent not even, indeed, for all that is not at least implicitly prohibited, but only for whatever is expressly permitted by the higher law, the constitutional form of the Church as established by Christ could be said to be exclusively monarchic. Accordingly, the Pope could so unlimitedly control and regulate the bishop's authority that he could thereby both theoretically and practically abolish the subordinate episcopate as a distinct juridical institute.[28] This, however, has been constantly and commonly repudiated by the doctrine of authors on the subject as an erroneous conception.[29]

Neither is the actual determination of the bishop's capacity by the Soverign Pontiff entirely arbitrary.[30] It is to be regulated according to the circumstances of time and locality, whether these are habitual or temporary, general or peculiar to a certain territorial section of the Universal Church. In other words, a just cause is required on the part of the Roman Pontiff in the limitation, restriction or conditioning of the bishop's authority. Ob-

[26] ". . . hinc limites maiores vel minores habere potest, *dummodo semper verificetur eos esse Pastores.*" —Cavagnis, *Institutiones Iuris Publici Ecclesiastici,* II, 474.

[27] "Quare Romanus Pontifex nec Episcoporum potestatem abrogare, nec eam adeo coarctare potest, ut fere inutilis evadat." —Solieri, *Institutiones Iuris Ecclesiastici,* p. 332.

[28] "Si confitendum est . . . Papam nullomodo posse abolere vel e medio tollere jurisdictionem Episcoporum *ordinariam,* fatemur nos intelligere non posse, qua ratione formam [i.e. Ecclesiae] possint hanc vocare simpliciter monarchicam, nisi verbis ludatur et ad umbram redigatur Episcoporum potestas *ordinaria.* Quare, si seligenda sit aliqua forma, haud incorrecte potest haec nominari *'monarchica aristocratico elemento coadjuvata'.*" —Bachofen, *Summa Iuris Ecclesiastici Publici,* pp. 44-45.

[29] Cavagnis, *Institutiones Iuris Publici Ecclesiastici,* II, 452-453; Ottaviani, *Institutiones Iuris Publici Ecclesiastici,* I, n. 212; Solieri, *Institutiones Iuris Ecclesiastici,* p. 332.

[30] Bachofen, *Summa Iuris Ecclesiastici Publici,* p. 25.

viously, it is the Pope himself who alone is competent to decide as to the existence of such a cause, and not the bishops whether collectively or individually.[31]

II. Positive Determination.

The aspects of the Papal power which directly occasion this operative dependence in all other authorities within the Church, including the episcopate, are its *supreme* and *immediate* qualities as defined in the Vatican Council.

In its character of an *immediate* quality, the Papal primacy of jurisdiction, which by reason of its universality extends to each and every ecclesiastical detail, is independent in its approach and may be directly applied. It alone is operatively free. Consequently, not only in extraordinary cases as claimed in the Febronian theories condemned by Pius VI,[32] but even in matters for which the ordinary power of the bishop is independently sufficient, can the Roman Pontiff intervene in the exercise of episcopal jurisdiction.

It has been seen in the foregoing discussion of the bishop's potential capacity in virtue of his native ordinary power that this capacity is basically determined by the so-called *causae maiores* either *essentiales* or *per se;* in other words, by that part of the common law concerning matters which by their nature are neither absolutely nor specifically diocesan issues, that is, which pertain to the universal Church antecedent to its diocesan divisions *(essentiales)* or which arise consequent to such territorial organization from the relation of the individual dioceses to the central authority or of one diocese to another *(per se)*. The greater portion of the existent common law, however, comprises what are known as the *causae maiores per accidens,* that is, matters which while they are potentially subject to the bishop's jurisdiction yet have been more or less actually subjected by positive

[31] " . . . potestas haec Episcoporum ita subjecta remanet, ut possit Papa eam restringere, mutare ac etiam adimere, *ex justa causa.* Quae justa causa an existat, judicium est penes eumdem Romanum Pontificem." —Bouix, *Tractatus de Episcopo,* I, 110.

[32] Brief "*Super soliditate,*" 28 nov. 1786, n. 4—*Fontes,* n. 473.

ecclesiastical legislation to the higher authority of the Pope in virtue of the *immediate* character of his jurisdictional primacy.[33]

This direct intervention on the part of the Sovereign Pontiff in otherwise episcopal questions may be evidenced in various ways, namely by *regulation, reservation, suspension* and *exemption.*[34] The purely regulative norms do not entirely nullify but rather definitely modify the bishop's ordinary power with reference to the matters he supervises by prescribing or prohibiting certain methods of official performance. Reservation,[35] however, implies a complete withdrawal of the matters reserved from the scope of the bishop's ordinary jurisdiction. Exemption means the habitual withdrawal of certain persons, places and things within the territorial limits of the diocese (and by nature potentially subject to the bishop) from the actual influence of the episcopal prerogatives, either wholly or partially. Suspension in the sense intended here means the anticipating of the bishop's action in any particular instance. It is evidenced rather in particular papal decrees relative to particular dioceses than in the common law. The decrees of plenary and provincial councils may also be included as examples of this suspension of the individual bishop's authority, since although these enactments are

[33] Cavagnis, *Institutiones Iuris Publici Ecclesiastici,* II. 439.

[34] "Quod enim possit Pontifex a jurisdictione episcoporum subtrahere certas res vel personas quae alias ad eam pertinerent pro certe habendum est. Nam etsi ius divinum sanxerit ut singuli greges episcopis tamquam ordinariis pastoribus regendi committerentur, adhuc tamen quaedam latitudo est intra quam episcopalis potestas restrictionem patitur, quin propterea desinat esse potestas ad pascendum populum Dei. Nec opportuit ut per ius divinum omnino immobiliter determinaretur id quod debuit manere aliqualiter mutationi obnoxium pro varietate circumstantiarum ac temporum, pro maiori vel minori facilitate recursus ad Sedem Apostolicam, aliisque eiusmodi. Nunc autem, si ius divinum non assignavit in individuo fines epicopalis potestatis, constat ipsam posse plus minusve restringi per ius pontificium, quia nullos alios limites novit pontificia auctoritas praeter eos quos ei ius divinum praefixit. Hinc ergo locum habent reservationes casuum, causarum, dispensationum, et similia." —Billot, *Tractatus De Ecclesia Christi* (5. ed, 2. vols., Romae: Apud Aedes Universitatis Gregorianae, 1927), I, 713.

[35] Conc. Trid., Sess. XIV, c. 7—Mansi, XXXIII, 96.

not specifically papal in all cases they nevertheless obtain their canonical force in every instance by papal recogntion.[36]

In itself the above described intervention in diocesan affairs by the Roman Pontiff constitutes a factor which on occasion militates against the general discretionary character of the bishop's ordinary power. The latter, however, cannot arbitrarily withstand, ignore, or go contrary to such intervention on the score that, in his own judgment (which, indeed, may be quite correct), the papal measures are, will be or have been less conducive than his own personl management of the reserved or exempted affairs would have been or could be for the needs that must be consulted in his diocese, and that consequently, without further ado, his own ideas of management are not only preferable but must actually supercede the former. This proposition was, indeed, at least insinuated at the Synod of Pistoia, but was naturally condemned as conducive to schism and branded as subversive of hierarchical government.[37] Such a condition would render the sovereign power of the Church subject to the subordinate in its practical application. The bishop may, of course, refer his opinion as to the utility of either a general or a particular enactment of a higher authority regarding his diocese to the Holy See, and either ask or suggest that special provision be allowed for his territory in accordance with the peculiar local circumstances existent there.[38] However,

36 Canon 291, § 1.

37 "Item quod et sibi persuasum esse ait, *iura episcopi a Iesu Christo accepta pro gubernanda Ecclesia, nec alterari, nec impediri posse; et ubi contigerit horum iurium exercitium quavis de causa fuisse interruptum, posse semper episcopum, ac debere in originaria sua iura regredi, quotiescumque id exigit maius bonum suae ecclesiae;* in eo quod innuit iurium episcopalium exercitium nulla superiori potestate praepediri, aut coerceri posse, quandocumque episcopus proprio iudicio censuerit minus id expedire maiori bono suae ecclesiae,—*Inducens in schisma, et subversionem hierarchici regiminis, erronea.*" —Pius VI, const. "*Auctorem fidei,*" 28 aug. 1794, n. 16 (propositio octava damnata) —*Fontes*, n. 475.

38 Benedict XIV, *De Synodo Dioecesana,* lib. 9, c. 8, nn. 2-4; "Generatim loquendo cum quilibet Episcopus catholicus unionem habens cum Sede Apostolica censeri debeat filius obediens Supremi Pontificis, si qua lex certo non est publicata in dioecesi, non obligare praesumitur fideles et clericos talis dioecesis" —Prümmer, *Manuale Iuris Canonici* (4. ed., Friburgi: Herder, 1927), n. 19.

until the Sovereign Pontiff, either personally or through the agency deputed by him to care for such affairs as are in question, has been consulted and has decided the matter, the individual bishop must practically defer his judgement and be guided by the existing law. On the other hand, if he prudently deems the positive intervention of the higher jurisdiction in any particular instance to be actually detrimental to the good government of his diocese, the bishop *must* so refer the matter to the superior authority; and if the gravity of the case so warrants he may meanwhile take provisional steps toward avoiding such harm as he fears may arise from the literal acceptance of the law in question.[39]

In the light of the foregoing statement concerning the dependence of episcopal jurisdiction on the papal primacy, there vanishes the possible difficulty[40] of conceiving two powers, each characterized as proper, ordinary, and immediate over the same territory, a difficulty which might seem to lead to the obvious conclusion that either the one or the other of the powers is not correctly so characterized. For there is no inevitable incompatibility between two such jurisdictions, if the one is actually subordinated to the other in such a way that there can be no real juridically legitimate opposition, so that in the case of conflict the one must prevail over the other.[41] There is, therefore, no juridical incongruity in the fact that both bishop and pontiff are the immediate superiors over the diocese, since the former is not independent of the latter.[42]

[39] Cf. Wernz, *Ius Decretalium,* I, 102; Coronata, *Institutiones Iuris Canonici* (5 vols., Taurini: Marietti, 1928-1936), I, n. 6.

[40] ". . . . est difficultas concipiendi duas potestates proprias, ordinarias et immediatas, in eodem territorio et in easdem personas, quae effecit ut quidam negarent potestatem ordinariam episcoporum et quidam Pontificis . . . "—Cavagnis, *Institutiones Iuris Publici Ecclesiastici,* II, 453.

[41] ". . . inconveniens esset, si duo aequaliter super eumdem gregem constituerentur; sed quod duo, quorum unus alio principalior est, super eamdem plebem constituantur, non est inconveniens; et secundum hoc super eamdem plebem *immediate* sunt et sacerdos parochialis et Episcopus et Papa . . . "—St. Thomas, *Comm. in IV Sent.* (Parisiis: Vivès, 1873), dist. XVII, q. III, a. III, q. 5.

[42] "Et vere repugnaret si utraque esset independens; sed cum episco-

This subordination is further emphasized in the relation of the episcopate to the papal primacy in the latter's character of a *supreme* quality. This note of the Roman Pontiff's jurisdiction over the whole Church bespeaks its exclusive operative finality and infers its efficacy as to both the veto, on the one hand, and the vindication, on the other, of all lesser authoritative action. Though the bishop is truly the supreme authority within his diocese, the finality of his jurisdiction is only relative in comparison with that of the Sovereign Pontiff. The primatial supremacy of the papal jurisdiction renders the episcopal power operatively subject to it. The need for functional unity in a perfect society demands this,[43] for as was said above, the actually existent common law at any given time will not exhaust the *de jure* possibilities, nor will that law clearly and precisely cover all the contingencies in which it may perhaps come to be invoked. Moreover, conditions may arise in particular dioceses for which the bishop can and possibly has provided as he deems expedient, but concerning which, because these same circumstances may arise later throughout other localities, it is thought necessary or useful that they be uniformly regulated for all eventualities. Thus, in virtue of his primatial supremacy the Pope can, either prior to or on occasion of recourse and appeal, revoke episcopal provisions and decisions, as well as ratify them. The episcopal power, then, is not absolutely final; but neither is it merely as strong as itself.[44] It is both corrigible and sustainable in virtue of a higher authority.[45]

porum potestas sit subordinata, nulla est repugnantia coexistentiae pastoris supremi et secundarii." —Cavagnis, *Institutiones Iuris Publici Ecclesiastici,* II, 453.

[43] "Quamvis populi distinguantur inter diversas dioeceses et civitates, tamen sicut est una Ecclesia, ita oportet esse unum populum Christianum. Sicut igitur in uno speciali populo unius Ecclesiae requiritur unus episcopus qui sit totius populi caput, ita in toto populo Christiano requiritur quod unus sit totius Ecclesiae caput."—St. Thomas, *Contra Gentiles,* lib.

[44] "Romani autem Pontifices . . . quemadmodum potestatem suam ea qua par est cura vigilantiaque tuentur, ita et dedere et dabunt constanter operam ut sua episcopis auctoritas salva sit." —Leo XIII, ep. encycl. *"Satis cognitum,"* 29 iun. 1896, n. 31 —*Fontes,* n. 630.

[45] "Tantum autem abest, ut haec Summi Pontificis potestas officiat ordi-

The supremacy of the papal jurisdiction suggests in addition its supervisory capacity to which the Gallicans and the Febronians would have reduced it entirely and exclusively. The Roman Pontiff has not only the right but the duty as well to see that the bishop rightly rules within the limits of his power. He has the right and the duty of inspection and direction. The bishop, moreover, must cooperate as to the one and at least react with deference to the other. This supervision may be exercised either directly or through intermediaries. The latter procedure is evidenced in the functions of the Roman Congregations, Tribunals, and Offices, as well as in that of apostolic legates and of metropolitans.

The somewhat singular rights which the metropolitan formerly enjoyed over his suffragans have been considerably curtailed. The prerogatives of the metropolitan as such are now comprehensively enumerated in the few provisions of canons 274 and 338 § 4 of the Code of Canon Law. Whatever their extent was or is, they never were and are not at the present time in any way prejudicial to the divinely constituted power of the bishop. They were and still are granted to the metropolitan in virtue of a supra-episcopal authority deputed to him by the Pope, and are therefore a manifestation of the Sovereign Pontiff's prerogative of inspective and directive supervision. Here, too, the positive intervention of the Pope in the function of episcopal government, through his legates or metropolitans, must not exceed the bounds of necessity, but must be determined by the good of the Church and in so far as demanded for its achievement.[46] Met-

nariae ac immediatae illi episcopalis jurisdictionis potestati, qua Episcopi, qui positi a Spiritu Sancto in Apostolorum locum successerunt, tamquam veri pastores assignatos sibi greges, singuli singulos, pascunt et regunt, *ut eadem a supremo et universali Pastore asseratur, roboretur, ac vindicetur,* secundum illud sancti Gregorii Magni: Meus honor est honor universalis Ecclesiae." Conc. Vat., Sess. IV, c. 3 —Denzinger-Bannwart, *Enchiridion,* n. 1828.

[46] "Cum potestas inferiorum pastorum ex divina ordinatione manet, nec ea ut otiosa sit aut inefficax fuerit concessa a Deo, quippe qui *eos posuit regere Ecclesiam Dei,* hinc per potestatem episcopalem eatenus limitem posuit Christus pontificiae potestati, vel potius eiusdem usui, ut non possit Papa Episcoporum jura ultra coercere, quam bonum Ecclesiae poscat, nec

ropolitans, therefore, as well as the other agencies employed by the Pope for the purpose of efficiency, vigilance or report, are intermediaries between him and the bishops. Their office is of purely ecclesiastical institution, their power is vicarious, and they are competent only for those matters and in those circumstances for which they are expressly empowered by the supreme authority. Otherwise, in the case of the metropolitan for instance, there would be verified the absurdity that one bishop, other than the bishop of Rome, could intervene on his own authority in the jurisdiction of another, a procedure which is not only illicit but invalid even in the most extraordinary circumstances, since the scope of episcopal jurisdiction—the objective comprehension of the individual bishop's authority discussed in the following chapter—is not dependent on or limitable by any other power than that of the Bishop of Rome.

However, even within the limits placed by positive ecclesiastical law upon the bishop's natural prerogatives, his authority is not absolute or arbitrary. It is intended for the maximum spiritual utility of those whom it governs, and is ordained in its use to the building up of the mystical body of Christ, not merely on the basis of legal uniformity or extremity and far less by force of official domination, but rather, and to a great extent, on the foundation of that paternal and pastoral care which alone can beget the trusting confidence and love of his spiritual children, one for another, of the flock for its shepherd, and unite them, as members of Christ's body, with the visible head of the Church.[47]

immodicis reservationibus, aut nimiis in vicarios apostolicos, nuntios ac legatos, collatis facultatibus, quodammodo exhaurire vel absorbere jurisdictionem Episcoporum." Zallinger, *Institutiones Iuris Naturalis et Ecclesiastici Publici* (3 vols., Romae, 1823), n. 359.

[47] "Atque huiusmodi potestas Episcopis est summa cum utilitate eorum in quos exercetur, data: spectat enim natura sua ad *aedificationem corporis Christi,* perficitque ut Episcopus quisque, cuiusdam instar vinculi, christianos, quibus praeest, et inter se et cum Pontifice maximo, tanquam cum capite membra, fidei caritatisque communione consociet." —Leo XIII, ep. encycl. *"Cum multa,"* 8 dec. 1882, n. 4—*Fontes,* n. 587; Benedict XIV, *De Synodo Dioecesana,* lib. 11, c. 7, n. 6.

CHAPTER V

THE OBJECTIVE COMPREHENSION

"Tum in spiritualibus tum in temporalibus"

Having indicated the operative competence of the residential bishop's ordinary authority to govern his diocese in the full sense of the term in virtue of his subjective capability, canon 335 states further that this competence embraces both the spiritual and the temporal diocesan affairs. In other words, it expresses the objective comprehension of diocesan government, the matter around which the bishop's power is exercisable, its material object. There is no question here of the juridical intensity of the bishop's power over any particular matter, but merely a question as to what matters the bishop's jurisdiction in one way or another and to some extent at least applies. Since the ordinary and proper potentiality of episcopal jurisdiction is specifically diocesan, the matters to which it applies must also in some way be specifically diocesan. Those matters are so characterized which have both a qualitative and at the same time a quantitative relation to diocesan government. That is to say, they must be of a certain kind and they must belong to a particular portion thereof. The kind or variety itself (i.e. the quality) depends on the essential purpose, whereas the portion or amount (i.e. the quantity) depends on the existential purpose of the diocese. In other words, the qualitative object of episcopal jurisdiction is contingent on the purpose common to the diocese and the Church of which it is a part, while the quantitative object is contingent on the purpose proper to a diocese as a part distinct from the whole Church.

Since the intended purpose of a diocese is merely the general purpose of the Church as locally particularized, it follows that the power of jurisdiction required for diocesan government must generically include as the *qualitatively* juridical matter over which it is to be exercised whatever concerns and is embraced by the general purpose of the Church. The individual bishop's jurisdiction, however, will be applicable only to that particular part of this general category which is *quantitatively* characterized as diocesan by reason of the distinct purpose of the episcopate in the jurisdictional hierarchy. This latter specification will be determined not only by the potential extent, but also by the actual limitation, of the bishop's power by papal reservations or exemption. The following treatment, then, will consider both the qualitative and the quantitative object of episcopal jurisdiction, the one as consequent to and the other as conditioned upon the general purpose of the Church.

Article I

Qualitative Object of Diocesan Government

Episcopal jurisdiction, like any species of social power, is primarily and directly concerned with the government of persons, since they are the immediate content of the social body. Just as the state is intended for the personal happiness of its subjects, so the ecclesiastical society is ordained to the personal holiness of its members. Moreover, it is mainly because of their habitual relation or circumstantial reference to the social members that other matters, real or actual, are subjected to jurisdictional control. It is necessary, therefore, to consider herein not only the so called material object, but also—and, indeed, first of all—the personal object of episcopal authority.

I. Personal Object.

The first requisite for subjection to any ecclesiastical jurisdiction is naturally membership in the ecclesiastical society. Membership in the Church and, as it were, automatic subordination to her authority is effected by the valid reception of Baptism, by which one is endowed with a juridical personality that is *per se* generative of all the rights and duties of a Christian.[1] Consequently, all validly baptized persons are *de iure* subject to the authority of the Church in general, and, given the conditions explained below, may also be *de iure* subject to this or that particullar bishop's jurisdiction, regardless of whether or not they are also *de facto* members of the Church, that is, in active external union with it.

[1] Canon 87.

The fundamental basis for the legitimate exercise of episcopal authority over a certain group or class of persons is nothing more or less than the territory itself of the diocese over which the bishop canonically presides.[2] The residential bishop's jurisdiction, as has been said in reference to his natively potential capability, is ultimately and radically territorial as to its purpose, and therefore it is also primarily territorial as to its content and extent. This is to say that, while episcopal authority is principally directed toward a personal object (for the sanctification of souls) and embraces all else by reason of a personal reference, it nevertheless affects its personal object through a territorial medium, by reason of a local association or bond. The stability of this bond is the norm which determines the actual degree of subjection, that is, whether it be *complete, partial, temporary*, or *permanent.* Thus, the more stable the personal connection with the locality, the greater the subordination to the local ordinary. It must be remembered that in speaking here of degrees of subjection to episcopal jurisdiction there is question not of intensity or extent, but only of the fact itself, whatever may be its practical import.

The regular inhabitants of a diocese *(incolae),* namely those who have established a domicile therein, are obviously the most *permanently* subject to episcopal jurisdiction.[3] Such are reasonably presumed as being definitely settled in the locality, and as absent therefrom only by way of exception. They, therefore, are the usual and ordinary subjects of diocesan jurisdiction, whatever their status or condition of life may be, unless they have been by the special privilege of exemption withdrawn therefrom.[4] They are those for whose spiritual welfare the institu-

[2] "Fundamentum legitimi exercitii episcopalis auctoritatis in certum populum certumque clerum est ipsum territorium dioecesanum cui Episcopus canonice praesidet." —S. C. C., 12 aug. 1871 —*ASS,* VI (1870-71), 587.

[3] Canon 92, § 1; "Quare omnes qui cum territorio sunt aliqua stabili ratione colligati, sive ratione originis et domicilii, sive ratione tantum domicilii, obnoxios regulariter esse eidem episcopali auctoritati." —S. C. C., 12 aug. 1871—*ASS,* VI (1870-71), 587.

[4] "Quod si quis legis *subjectum,* ut aiunt, hoc est personas inquirat quae

tion of the episcopate as a territorial authority was intended by Christ, and whom, as a result, diocesan divisions and organization in the Church naturally and primarily regard. They consequently are also the most *completely* subject to episcopal jurisdiction. By reason, therefore, of their supposedly permanent affiliation with the territory which he governs, they naturally come under the full spiritual jurisdiction of the diocesan bishop,[5] who has in favor of his authority over them the general principle of an intention founded in law which perdures in full practical force unless and until it is clearly proved that this or that individual or class has been privileged by exemption or that the bishop's native power has been limited in their regard.[6] In cases of doubt, moreover, the same rule favoring the bishop's potential authority must always be observed until an exception is proved by the claimant.[7] Between those who fall into this category of natural diocesan subjects there is no essential distinction between lay and clerical, secular or religious, regarding the completeness of the bishop's native power over them. The diocesan clergy, of course, are more permanently bound since they cannot, like the laity, withdraw themselves from subjection

Dioecesanae Synodi decretis ligentur, paucis respondetur verbis, ad eorundem observationem adigi quotquot *incolunt* Episcopi dioecesim, cuiuscumque sint status et conditionis, nisi speciali privilegio ab eiusdem subtrahantur jurisdictione." —Benedict XIV, *De Synodo Dioecesana,* lib. 13, c. 4, n. 5.

[5] Although not so permanently, nevertheless just as completely subject to the bishop's authority are those who maintain merely a quasidomicile *(advenae)* in his diocese according to the norm of the positive law (Canon 92, §2).

[6] "Quemlibet ordinarium plena ex iure gaudere spirituali jurisdictione super omnes personas morantes intra fines Dioecesis a Romano Pontifice sibi concreditae. Ideoque huiusmodi jurisdictionem Antistitis cuiuslibet habentis fundatam in iure intentionem et generalem regulam in sui favorem, integram permanere donec allegans limitationem aut exemptionem per lucidis probaverit argumentis." —S. C. Ep. et Reg., 23 ian. 1880 —*ASS* X (1880), 30.

[7] "In dubio an exemptio exstet, regulae generali semper inhaerendum esse, donec exceptio probetur eo qui exemptionem allegat." —S. C. Ep. et Reg., 23 ian. 1880 —*ASS,* X (1880), 30.

to the bishop merely by voluntary transfer to another region. They are held by the added bond of ministerial service to the diocese.[8]

In regard to the aforementioned regularly established dwellers within the diocesan boundaries, the jurisdiction of the residential bishop is at once both *personal* and *territorial*. This means that while the bishop's authority over them, as his diocesans in the fullest sense, rests as explained above on a territorial basis, it is nevertheless not exclusively restricted as to the fact itself by territorial bounds. That is to say, it is strictly territorial in its origin, but not entirely territorial as to its extent. Although the bishop's jurisdiction over them is complete and permanent because, in view of their local stability, they live for the most part at least within the diocesan limits, he may somewhat exercise his power over them even when they are not actually present in the diocese.[9] The basis for this extra-diocesan extension of episcopal jurisdiction over such as are intimately connected with the diocese by so habitual a bond as customary residence is both social and individual.

The *social* reason is that the parties in question, although physically absent therefrom, may nevertheless, because of their recognizedly close association therewith, actually affect, howsoever slightly, the repute and influence the social order of their native diocese. They may and at times must, therefore, be considered as morally present therein, and consequently on occasion and in some regards at least are necessarily subjectable to the juridic control of the authority responsible for the diocesan welfare, even though both they and he be beyond the local limits of his jurisdictional prerogatives. The *individual* reason is that those persons who maintain regular residence in the diocese have been particularly accredited and entrusted to the spiritual charge of the bishop thereof for the furtherance of their individual

[8] S. C. C., 12 aug. 1871 —*ASS*, VI (1870-71), 587.

[9] "Jurisdictio Episcopi est simul personalis et territorialis, scil., personae fiunt ipsi subjectae mediante territorio, at in eas postea exercetur eius auctoritas, saltem quoad quaedam, etiam extra dioecesim." —Rivet, *Institutiones Iuris Ecclesiastici Privati* (Romae, 1914), I, 383.

sanctification, which is, in fact, the first and final purpose of his office and power. Since neither the purpose nor the process of sanctification ceases by the fact of their temporary absence from the territorial pale of the bishop's authority, his jurisdiction cannot properly be entirely suspended thereby. It must, in view of its purpose, be capable of affecting them when necessary for their spiritual good even though they are absent from their diocesan domicile, since their individual spiritual welfare may not always be identified with the social good of their particular diocese as such.

There are, on the other hand, some persons over whom the bishop's jurisdiction is strictly *territorial and temporary,* though it may at the same time be either partial or complete. It is *territorial only* because it is caused by and conditioned upon their actual presence in the diocese and persists only for the duration of their physical stay therein. It is *temporary* because their actual presence is temporary, since they have no permanent residential tie or link to the locality. Their presence within the diocese, in other words, is merely accidental or circumstantial. Its juridical significance or import, however, varies according to the relative stability of their local connections elsewhere. If they happen to have no stable abode anywhere, but are simply vagrants *(vagi),* their actual presence in any particular diocese is comparatively permanent in the sense that it is as lasting there as anywhere. In this case, both the social order of the universal Church as well as their own individual spiritual welfare demand that they be to the *maximum possible* extent subject to the jurisdictional authority in the place of their actual sojourn, since that is the only authority which can at any given time and in any given place practically serve the purpose of the Church in their regard. The bishop's jurisdiction over them is by the very nature of their status as complete during their stay in his diocese as it is in regard to his habitual subjects.[10]

If, on the contrary, they have a permanent home elsewhere *(peregrini),* they are by that fact the ordinary object of their

[10] Canons 94, § 2; 14, § 2; Van Hove, *De Legibus Ecclesiasticis,* n. 224.

proper bishop's jurisdiction and, though they be actually absent from his territory, they remain virtually subject to the authority of him who governs in their place of habitual residence, because they have been substantially committed to his care. They are, however, the actual extraordinary subjects of the bishop who rules the locality in which they at present happen to be. For, since their presence and conduct while there may affect and influence the social order, they must necessarily on occasion be liable to control by the social authority thereof. However, their status as the ordinary subjects of another jurisdiction and as merely accidental subjects of this one requires that their subjection to the latter extend only to the *minimum necessary*. The residential bishop's authority over them, therefore, is not only strictly territorial and temporary, but it is also only partial.[11] In this category of persons who are circumstantially subject to episcopal jurisdiction must be included those otherwise exempted therefrom by privilege of the positive law, whether they be in the diocese where they habitually reside or in another. The natural interests of the diocesan social order as interpreted by the bishop must ultimately prevail over other considerations of acquired status or conferred dignity. Consequently, on occasion of incompatibility, by reason, for instance, of scandal or example fraught with the danger of resultant disregard for episcopal authority by others who are subject to it, conformity to those interests is demanded even at the expense of immunity otherwise enjoyed.[12]

Thus the authority of the residential bishop is by its very nature habitually and completely inclusive of some, while it is circumstantially and partially comprehensive of other persons. It remains to discuss the material object, that is, the matters which in reference to the above-mentioned persons fall under the scope of episcopal jurisdiction.

[11] In practice this principle is by positive law (canon 14, § 1, n. 2) applied only to matters which are rather preventive of social difformity than productive of social benefit.

[12] "Aliquando ad evitandum scandalum et fugiendam difformitatem a ceteris dioeceseos membris teneri regulares obtemperare Constitutionibus synodalibus, a quibus ceteroquin, ratione suae exemptionis, essent soluti . . . "—Benedict XIV, *De Synodo Dioecesana,* lib. 13, c. 4, n. 5.

II. Material Object.

Since the jurisdictional office of the Church, in which as has been seen the bishop as a principal participant fully shares, is to teach Christian belief and to rule Christian behaviour, the jurisdictional object of the residential bishop's office may be aptly divided and general determined within its proper bounds according to these two aspects of ecclesiastical jurisdiction, the doctrinal and the disciplinary.

1. Doctrinal Matter.

The bishop's power in accord with its purpose is essentially spiritual, and its scope must therefore be essentially spiritual also. Since that purpose is ultimately the sanctification and salvation of souls, the teaching authority of the residential bishop must extend to all the *known* truths of the spiritual order, since the spiritual is the proper and exclusive realm of the Church as a spiritual kingdom, working to the salvation of souls, spiritual entities.

His primary concern, like that of the Church which he officially represents, is therefore with the deposit of faith, the body of revealed truths which Christ and the Holy Spirit made known to the apostles. His is an apostolic office with an apostolic object, and this connotes first of all the whole content of Christian revelation, as found in Scripture and Tradition and as proposed by the infallible authority of the Church. These are the supernatural truths, the mysteries or religion.

Although these truths do not comprise the whole doctrinal content of the spiritual order, it is in regard to them precisely that the jurisdiction of the Church in general and of the bishop in particular has a more extensive application than in other matters either doctrinal or disciplinary. For the exercise of the bishop's doctrinal jurisdiction over matters of pure faith must be concerned with more than the teaching of his actual subjects. That is to say, the bishop's doctrinal right and duty entails not only the teaching of the faith to those who are both *de iure* and *de facto* members of the Church, but also the propagation of the faith in those who are in either sense outside the fold.[13] The personal object of the bishop's office in regard to the mysteries of faith, therefore, includes not only the Catholic but also the non-Catholic, whether Christian or non-Christian, members of his diocese.

The truths of the spiritual order, however, are not restricted to or comprehensively contained in revelation. Nor do they include only those verities which are rather speculative than practical. There are others which reason alone can deduce, and there are many which bear directly on external behaviour. In other words, there are philosophical as well as theological dogmas pertinent to the spiritual order, and there is the so-called naturally known as well as the positively proposed moral truth. All these are part of the spiritual order and are primarily and directly involved in the salvation of souls. They consequently unite with the truths of revelation to form the object of the bishop's teaching authority. This object, therefore, may be said to extend to and to embrace, as does that of the universal Church, all dogmatic and moral truths whether these are based on Christian belief in the strict sense of the term or on what may be called Christian reason.

However, although there may be no question of the bishop's right and duty to teach on purely spiritual questions, although there may be ready assent to the abstract doctrine that he is the authorized teacher of faith and morals, of Christian belief and ethics, the practical application of that doctrine to concrete matters may often present some difficulty. There are questions which evidently and obviously lie within the spiritual sphere. There are others which just as apparently lie beyond that sphere. In these latter the bishop himself will claim no right to teach authoritatively. They are purely temporal, secular or material, and the bishop has no direct official commission to communicate profane knowledge as such, howsoever, well-versed he may personally happen to be in the various sciences. He has not been sent to teach them. They are not part of the gospel entrusted to

[13] Canon 1350, § 1.

him as his apostolic legacy, since the end and aim of the Church is not a temporal or material one, but the spiritual betterment of all its members in view of eternal life.

There is a third class of questions, however, a wide field of matters of mixed spiritual and temporal significance. Some of them are primarily and of themselves spiritual but with a definite reference to the temporal, in so far as certain temporal considerations are not only frequently conducive to but even always necessary for the practical prosecution of the Church's proper work. Others are in themselves temporal, but with a spiritual side in that they involve moral issues on occasion at least. If the spiritual and the temporal happened always to stand totally apart, no dispute would be possible as to the boundaries of episcopal authority in doctrinal affairs. As a matter of fact, however, the temporal and the spiritual are so intermingled as to overlap. There is, that is to say, in the complexity of human life, no well-defined dividing line between the two spheres. There are numerous questions in which the spiritual and the temporal are interwoven inextricably. It is regarding these mixed matters that the bishop has doctrinal jurisdiction over truths of the temporal order, in virtue and to the extent of the Church's indirect power over such matters.[14]

The bishop, therefore, has unquestionable and direct power to teach and to pronounce on wholly spiritual principles, and none whatever over purely temporal tenets. In those of a mixed nature he has direct authority over the spiritual and indirect authority over the temporal element by reason of its connection with the spiritual. Although the authority of Church rulers does not extend to material or temporal things taken precisely as such, it does extend to material or temporal things in so far as they have a bearing on the spiritual, in so far, that is, as they must be

[14] "Per potestatem indirectam intelligimus illam quae non directe et principaliter ratione sui ordinis exercetur, sed propter connexionem insep arabilem cum alio. Ideoque dicimus quod potestas in spiritualia directe et principaliter Ecclesiae competit, in temporalia indirecte et secundario, seu ex consequenti et ratione peccati."—Paris, *De Ecclesia Christi* (Taurini: Marietti, 1929), 192.

influenced by it or must exercise an influence on the spiritual so as either to impede or to help the achievement of salvation.[15]

There are but few branches or problems of profane knowledge whose principles do not involve some reference to the spiritual, at least in so far as their application involves or can involve a moral issue. Whenever the conscience enters, the Church enters. Consequently in questions concerning any and every department of life where a moral issue can emerge, in political, scientific, commercial, literary, artistic, recreational affairs, the Church and so the bishop have the right and duty to present with authoritative voice the truth of the matter as to when and where there is or can be a question of proper principles either of belief or of behavior.[16] This, as regards the doctrinal object of episcopal jurisdiction, is the meaning of the canon when it states that the bishop's prerogative of government extends to both spiritual and temporal matters. The same prerogative applies similarly to disciplinary affairs, concerning which the foregoing is applicable, though in a somewhat different manner.

2. Disciplinary Matter.

The exercise of the bishop's doctrinal right is immediately ordained to and effective of a mental or internal assent on the part of those whom he teaches. It thus accomplishes a purely spiritual condition, and one which in itself is entirely a matter of the internal forum. An act of pure faith, for instance, not only concerns a truth which is spiritual in that either wholly or partially it has direct or indirect reference to the spiritual welfare and destiny of man, but the physical act itself as a psychological reality is spiritual or immaterial in that it is the product of a spiritual entity, the soul. The truths which are so accepted and adhered to, however, are not entirely matters of pure belief in the sense that they terminate therein. Faith without works is dead because the truths of faith as well as the truths of reason connected with it all have some reference to practical behaviour. Many of them demand a certain outward performance, while others definitely

[15] Cf. Turrecremata, *Summa de Ecclesia* (Venetiis, 1561).

[16] Leo XIII, ep. encycl. "*Immortale Dei,*" 1 nov. 1885, n. 27 —*Fontes* n. 592.

modify exterior performance whencesoever it is motivated. External conformity with these truths, therefore, is a requisite of salvation, and it itself is a matter of the external forum.

The Church, then, as the agency through which men are to work out their salvation, has the right and the duty to regulate external acts. These are the direct object of the bishop's disciplinary authority, in so far as they pertain to the whole practical life of the Christian as such. They will include, first of all, those acts which relate to the direct practice of faith, such as the formal worship of God, the reception of the Sacraments, as well as all that immediately concerns the concrete application of Christian belief and reason to everyday life, the observance of the Christian precepts and counsels. All these, though they entail visible and corporeal action, are of themselves spiritual, since they refer exclusively to the spiritual advancement of man as their prime purpose.

All that was said above concerning purely temporal matters applies also to the disciplinary object of episcopal jurisdiction. The bishop, in other words, has no direct official interest in such affairs, howsoever adept he may personally be in regulating them. Applicable too, as above explained, is the principle of the indirect power of the Church over temporal matters in so far as they are capable of becoming the agencies of spiritual acts, virtues and vices. Therefore, because of the complexity of human activity in which the spiritual and the temporal are for the most part practically inseparable, the bishop's disciplinary authority will extend to whatever, though temporal in itself, involves a spiritual issue, whether always or only in given circumstances and conditions. Thus, because in almost every visible, external, corporeal action there may possibly be a moral content or relation, the whole sphere of human life may likewise possibly be the object of episcopal authority,[17] to the extent demanded for the security of the moral or spiritual issue.[18]

[17] "Quia fere tota materia temporalis ad spiritualem finem ordinari potest, et illi subest, sub illo respectu inducit quamdam rationem spiritualis materiae, et ita potest ad leges canonicas pertinere." —Suarez, *Tractatus de Legibus*, lib. 11, c. 11, n. 9.

[18] "Verum tamen iurisdictio Episcoporum non modo in iis exercetur

Included in the temporalities which are subject to the bishop's disciplinary authority are not only external acts but also material property, or what may be called the temporal goods of the Church. This involves, first of all, the real movable or immovable possessions already acquired and held as belonging to the Church in the diocese, by virtue of her native right as a perfect society either as a whole[19] or as to her particular juridical divisions.[20] It embraces furthermore whatever material property, although not yet actually owned or possessed by the Church, is absolutely necessary for her proper existence and function in the diocese. Since certain temporal or material conditions are naturally postulated for the Church precisely as a society and as distinguished from its individual members, the Church has a consequent right to require and obtain from her subjects the material contributions from their own private wealth which are essential to the achievement of her purpose in the environment in which she must exist and work. The bishop, therefore, has jurisdiction over the temporal goods of his subjects in so far as the welfare of the diocese absolutely and essentially demands.[21] This power is indirect and due to the spiritual reference and significance which such things do or may contain.

The qualitative object of episcopal jurisdiction, therefore, is rather comprehensive, coordinate as it is with that of the general power of the Church. It is, however, *quantitatively limited,* and necessarily so because of the natural subordination of the episcopal to the papal authority. Moreover because of the positive dependence of the episcopal on the papal authority it is also *quantitatively limitable.*

quae ad religiosas et ecclesiasticas res pertinent, sed in ceteris etiam quaestionibus cuiusvis naturae, quae directe vel indirecte cum Ecclesiae sanctae emolumento animarumque salute conjunguntur."—Benedict XV, *Epistola ad Delegatum Apostolicum in Indiis Orientalibus,* 15 oct. 1921 —*ASS,* XIV (1922), 8.

[19] Canon 1495, § 1; Ottavinai, *Institutiones Iuris Publici Ecclesiastici,* I, 198-204.

[20] Canon 1495, § 2.

[21] Canon 1496; Schultes, *De Ecclesia Catholica,* pp. 344-354.

Article II

Quantitative Object of Diocesan Government

The quantitative object of episcopal jurisdiction must not be confused with its juridical intensity. The former merely signifies that particular category within the general qualitative sphere of episcopal power which, in view of its precise purpose, the potentiality of that authority actually comprehends and to which it is specifically limited.

It has been stated that the operative competence of the residential episcopate, as demanded by it purpose, entails the complete government of a diocese. As was also said above, the government of a diocese does not essentially differ in its import from that of the universal Church. Consequently, as was finally seen in the immediately preceding article, the qualitative object of episcopal jurisdiction must be generically identified with that of ecclesiastical authority as a whole. However, although the qualitative object is in this sense determined as consequent to the purpose of the Church in general, it must naturally be specifically determined according to the specifically characteristic purpose of diocesan government, on the one hand, and positively conditioned upon the social welfare of the universal Church on the other. Within the spiritual and temporal sphere to which it pertains, as explained in the foregoing article, the authority of the diocesan bishop is first of all naturally and radically limited by its native *raison d'etre* and secondly it is also positively or functionally limitable for the necessary advantage of the universal Church. It is, then, by these specific qualitative limitations that the quantitative object of episcopal jurisdiction is and must be determined.

The natural subordination of the episcopate to the papacy, resulting from the absolute primacy of the latter, designates the potential capability of the former as specifically diocesan in virtue of its intended purpose in the jurisdictional hierarchy of the Church as established by Christ. This means that the qualitative object of episcopal jurisdiction is somehow basically restricted by those matters which are either essentially or by radical neces sity dependent on and reserved to the supreme power of the pontificate. These matters are not only those which are definitely actualized in law and which when so constituted must of necessity be contained in the common law as *causae maiores essentiales* or *per se (de iure reservanda et de facto reservata),* but also those matters which, though not yet actually constituted as such, must if and when they are so established be thus instituted by and pertain to the pontifical power *(de facto reservanda quia de iure reservata).* Such major issues may concern either the law of belief or the law of behaviour *(lex credendorum et agendorum).*

Moreover, the natural dependence of the episcopate in its actual function on the papal power and the positive determination of the former by the latter according to the demands of the universal Church further restrict that qualitative object. The matters thus limitative of the episcopal authority are those which are contained in the remainder of the common law or in particular pontifical laws relating to the diocese. They constitute the so called *causae maiores per accidens,* since they are not by their nature itself but rather by force of circumstances pontifical rather than episcopal *(de iure reservabilia et de facto reservata).*

The primary quantitative specification of episcopal authority, therefore, is twofold. It is the essential and the radically necessary common law, whether actual or merely potential. This specifies that which is not absolutely and exclusively diocesan by nature. The secondary quantitative specification of the residential bishop's power is likewise twofold. It is what may be called the accidental common law as well as particular papal law relative to the diocese, whether the latter is proper to the territory or common to several including it, such as the law of plenary or provincial councils. This specifies that which, although by nature diocesan, is not in virtue of positive decree absolutely and exclusively episcopal. Thus, the entire content of pontifical law which is either common to all or only to several dioceses, but including the one in question, or proper to the latter quantitatively restricts the sphere of episcopal jurisdiction.

It does so, however, as is apparent, in a negative way: by specifying what is not precisely episcopal. This must not be understood, however, in the sense that the matters determined as above described are entirely excluded from the sphere of the bishop's authority. They definitely concern the diocese, howsoever extensive they may otherwise be, and consequently pertain to and are entailed by diocesan government. Therefore, while they are not originally episcopal in their institution, they are existentially diocesan, and must ultimately in some way be episcopal also,[22] since the bishop must govern his diocese in accordance with them, as the canon itself explicitly states *("ad norman sacrorum canonum")*.

The quantitative object of diocesan government, therefore, includes these matters in the absolute sense that the bishop has some degree of jurisdiction in their regard. The positive significance of this fact pertains to the following discussion on the actual capacity of episcopal jurisdiction. Its import for this present consideration is, as was said, rather a negative one. For while it expressly determines some matters as reserved to the higher authority of the Pope, it equivalently denotes that whatever is *contrary* to them is thereby excluded from the realm of the bishop's power. Whatever contravenes or is opposed to the content of these laws, whether explicitly or implicitly, is beyond the pale of episcopal authority. This is the least that is demanded by the hierarchical relation of the two powers, since otherwise this relation could neither be theoretically conceived or practically maintained.

Regarding such matters, since the residential bishop's jurisdiction must be in accord with them *(secundum ius)* and not contrary *(contra ius)*, it may be said that his authority is contained altogether within and under the common papal law. It is not at all sufficient, however, to characterize the entire episcopal power in this way and to say simply, as some do, that the bishop's authority is wholly contained within and under the common law. While

[22] "Verum cum sibi proposita sit rei catholicae tutela et amplificatio, resque catholica in Dioecesibus singulis ab Episcopo geratur, sponte consequitur, eas Episcopis subesse et ipsorum auctoritati auspiciisque tribuere plurimum opportere."—Leo XIII, ep. encycl. *"Cum multa sint,"* 8 dec. 1882, n. 6 —*Fontes*, n. 587.

this statement is somewhat correct,[23] it is not comprehensive. In the first place it obviously ignores the particular pontifical laws, and thus fails to restrict the bishop's jurisdictional object sufficiently. In the second place, it makes no distinction between the two essentially different categories of the common law, and thus fails to extend the ambit of the episcopal power sufficiently.

It is, indeed, true that the bishop's jurisdictional object, considered as precisely relative to the matter which pertains to the essential and the radically necessary common law, is entirely contained within and under *(intra et sub)* it. This, however, must be understood as meaning that, while as to its quantitative object (and therefore with some degree of intensity, as will be seen in the following chapter) the bishop's authority includes such major items, the latter cannot, because of its naturally restricted potentiality, directly and positively include that which is beyond in the sense that it is contrary to *(ultra et supra sed contra)* the common law of this kind. In so far, however, as the bishop's authority embraces that which is in accord with such matters *(secundum ius)*, it does and at the same time must extend negatively and indirectly, so to speak, to whatever is not in agreement therewith, in the sense that the bishop's power must be directed to the exclusion of all that is contrary to the higher law.

All other matters beyond this category of the common law, on the contrary, fall directly within the sphere of the bishop's natural capability. Many of them, those which are embodied in the so-called accidental common law (as well as in particular pontifical law given for the diocese), are actually withdrawn to some extent from the bishop's positive operative competence and to the same juridical effect explained above regarding the primary common law. Concerning such matters, however, it is not enough to designate the bishop's jurisdictional object as *entirely* contained within and under the law. It cannot include what is contrary

[23] Cf., e.g., Cappello: "Iurisdictio Episcopi tota continetur *intra* et *sub* iure communi, tum quoad ambitum, tum quoad exercitium, ita ut nihil omnino Episcopus agere valeat contra illud ius . . ."—*Summa Iuris Canonici,* I, 455.

and must include what is according to these laws. The laws themselves, however, are not precisely natural restrictions, but merely positive limitations on the bishop's jurisdiction. In this sense they must be considered as relatively odious and consequently their juridical import is reduced to the necessary minimum. Therefore, although episcopal authority does not directly embrace what is opposed to the *per accidens* common law and particular papal decree, it does naturally include whatever is *beyond* in the sense that while, on the one hand, it is not expressly contrary nor, on the other, *substantially* according to the law, it is nevertheless altogether compatible with it *(praeter ius)*.

These latter matters are those which are both by nature and by positive law specifically diocesan since, being neither naturally nor positively characterized as pontifical, they are left to the residential bishop's jurisdiction, and unless otherwise expressly determined they are necessarily included in a very special manner within the sphere of its quantitative object.[24] They constitute the precisely determinate reason for the establishment of the episcopate in the Church as a complete juridical institute distinct from the papacy. The institute, moreover, was also occasioned and indeed necessitated by the practical demand for unity as to basic doctrine and discipline throughout the entire Church, so that the matters of the higher law which refer to this belief and behaviour have together with their universal import a specific diocesan significance and application, and must therefore also be included within the quantitative object of diocesan government, although, as will be immediately seen, not according to the same functional capacity.

The only absolute quantitative specification of the object of diocesan government, then, is that episcopal authority does not directly and positively include what is either substantially or modally, contrary to the law of the higher authority.

[24] "Haec Episcoporum potestas nullos habet fines, nisi generales Ecclesiae leges et peculiaria Pontificum decreta. Idcirco quae neque per generales Ecclesiae leges neque per peculiaria Pontificum decreta constituta sint, ea Episcoporum subjacent potestati." —Signatura Apostolica, 13 iun. 1923 —*AAS*, XVI (1924), 107.

Within this limitation, therefore, the quantitative object of episcopal jurisdiction is co-extensive with that of the Church as a whole. It potentially embraces whatever may possibly qualify as of ecclesiastical concern, whether directly because it is in itself spiritual or indirectly because, although temporal of itself, it has a spiritual import or reference. However, as was previously stated, even in matters which in general fall within both the potential and the actual scope of his jurisdiction, the bishop's authority is neither absolute or arbitrary. Since it is coordinate to the general power of the Church, episcopal jurisdiction is quantitatively determined in the concrete according to the same measure as ecclesiastical jurisdiction in general is determined. The Church as a juridically perfect society has social power in regard to *all* and *only* that which is either *absolutely requisite* or *relatively necessary* (useful) for the attainment of the social end or purpose.[25] The Church has been given authority with a view toward the immediate sanctification and the ultimate salvation of men, according to the norm established by Christ, namely, in virtue of membership in His Church through the agency of Baptism which constitutes them *Christians*. It is, therefore, precisely as *Christians* that the Church, through its bishops, directly governs its members according to the measure and extent demanded by their varied states and conditions of life. Consequently, whatever does not qualify as *Christian*, either *per se* or *per accidens*, this is, either by reason of content or consequence, does not pertain to the *potential* scope of episcopal jurisdiction. Moreover, unless such a Christian matter has, either essentially or circumstantially, a social significance, that is, unless it is either necessary or useful for the achievement of the Church's purpose, it does not pertain to the *actual* scope of episcopal authority.

[25] Cf. Solieri, *Institutiones Iuris Ecclesiastici*, p. 146.

Chapter VI

THE ACTUAL CAPACITY

"Cum potestate legislativa, judiciaria, coactiva ad normam sacrorum canonum exercenda"

The final statement of canon 335 is to the effect that the residential bishop has legislative, judicial and coactive power which must be exercised according to canonial norm. The phrase itself conveys a twofold concept. The first is suggested by the various species of power which are enumerated and concerns the practical integrity of the episcopal power, that is, what specific activity is entailed in the exercise of the bishop's office. The second notion involves the canonical norms which bind the bishop in the use of his official prerogatives and this concerns the positive intensity of the episcopal authority, that is, the force with which his official rights are endowed relative to the several activities for which he is practically competent. The canonical norms referred to may possibly be taken as inclusive of all the statutes of ecclesiastical law with which the bishop may have to deal in the detailed exercise of his office. Such a survey, however, is entirely beyond the purpose of a treatise on public law. Consequently, only those norms are considered herein which are pertinent by reason of a definite reference which they bear to the various aspects of episcopal government in action from the immediate standpoint of either doctrinal or disciplinary principles. The discussion which follows, therefore, will treat first of all the question of practical integrity, and secondly that of the positive intensity of episcopal jurisdiction, the one from the standpoint of social necessity, the other from that of the jurisdictional force required for effective diocesan government.

Article I

Practical Integrity of Episcopal Jurisdiction

The question considered here is twofold, that of the substantial faculties and that of the modal functions of episcopal power. The former has been all but completely discussed in a previous chapter, so that it will be sufficient at this point to treat of it onlv in so far as is necessary to distinguish it from the latter, which is the main issue under the present title.

I. Substantial Faculties.

The office of the bishop, because it is essentially apostolic, is generically one in itself, namely, the government of a diocese. However, since diocesan government is essentially identical with that of the universal Church, the office of the residential bishop is specifically twofold in its immediate purpose, namely, the proper belief and the correct behaviour of his subjects. Just as the episcopate is directed to the same official end as the apostolate, so it is also possessed of the same ordinary power which is likewise generically one in itself, that is, it is social. Moreover, just as the official end is specifically twofold, so the ordinary power comprises two specific faculties the general use of which constitutes the bishop's operative competence, as previously considered. It was seen then that the bishop's office is endowed with the two operative faculties required for essentially complete ecclesiastical authority, the doctrinal and the disciplinary. Consequently, as compared with ecclesiastical jurisdiction as a whole, the episcopal power is, so to speak, substantially perfect or integral. Just as the human soul, simple in itself, is possessed of two separate substantial faculties, the mental and the voluntary, so episcopal jurisdiction, though one in its ultimate aim, namely, the government of a diocese, nevertheless involves two distinct substantial faculties for its proximate operation. However, it is necessary to distinguish these faculties themselves from their actual use of function. This distinction between faculty and function (or, if the terms seem preferable, between substantial and modal function) is important not only as regards the functional integrity but also as regards the positive intensity of episcopal jurisdiction.

II. Modal Functions.

The word *function* is here differentiated from the term *faculty* in that it has a modal rather than a substantial significance. It refers to the particular kind of activity which is evidenced in the use of the episcopal powers and which unites, so to speak, the operative competence and the objective comprehension of the bishop's social authority. In virtue of its operative competence *(potestas facultativa)* the episcopate is empowered to rule or govern with both doctrinal and disciplinary effect. By reason of its objective comprehension the episcopate is capable of ruling or governing certain persons and things both as to doctrine and as to discipline. In order to pursue its purpose at all, however, its right and its object must in some way meet. The actual manner in which its right and its object meet, by which its power is coordinated to its purpose by application to its object, is properly called the *modal function* of the episcopate, which is therefore distinguished from its substantial faculties as the use or exercise of a power is distinguished from the power itself.

By *functional integrity,* therefore, is signified the completeness of specific activity necessary for the perfectly effective union of the operative competence and the legitimate object of episcopal jurisdiction. Moreover, since the bishop's authority is a substantially perfect participation in the power of a perfect society, it is naturally as regards such a society that the integrity of his jurisdictional activity or modal function must be measured.

All exercise of power possessed by a juridically perfect society in the completeness necessary to it as such is reduced to and requires three functions. Means to the social end must be devised and proposed. They must be interpreted and vindicated. They must be applied and enforced. To these three relations of the social means to the social end corresponds the threefold functional species of the social power in regard to these means: namely, the legislative, the judicial, and the executive.[1]

The full use or exercise of substantially perfect ecclesiastical jurisdiction *(potestas facultativa docendi et regendi)* requires each and all of these functions *(potestas functionalis legislativa, judiciaria, executiva)* and only these three. Consequently, if episcopal jurisdiction is capable of manifesting itself accordingly, it is also functionally integral. As a matter of fact, moreover, it

[1] Cf. Aristotle, *Politica* (Berlin: Reimer, 1831-1870), IV, 11.

is precisely because the intrinic faculties of episcopal power are essentially and substantially perfect that episcopal jurisdiction must be also functionally integral, that is, it must be characterized by a perfection of external operability. Otherwise the substantial perfection of the bishop's power is useless. It is inconceivable that a power be essentially perfect and at the same time functionally imperfect as to its native capability. Unless the functional capability of a power be perfect the power itself cannot be considered perfect, and conversely if the power be substantially perfect its functional capability cannot be otherwise. *Actio sequitur esse.* Operative capacity follows upon essence not only in the order of existence but also in the order of kind. There must, therefore, be a due proportion not only between a substance and its operation but also between the substance and the mode by which its faculties are used.[2] Episcopal power is essentially perfect in the jurisdictional order, and since there must be a due proportion between the mode and the nature of jurisdiction, the function of episcopal power must likewise be complete or integral in the jurisdictional order.[3] Moreover, while the functional potentiality native to episcopal jurisdiction may, like its facultative potentiality, be positively restricted and conditioned by the papal power, nevertheless, in regard to the power of those bishops who are necessary by reason of the divine institution of the episcopate and whose authority must be substantially perfect, the perfection of functional operability natively possessed must remain positively capable of perfect actualization. The latter, then, is by its very

[2] "Operatio tam perfecte et excellenter circa obiectum suum versatur quam perfecta est essentia operantis. Hinc proportio intercedere debet inter naturam operantis et modum, quo per operationem obiectum attingitur. . .Proportio etiam debet esse inter naturam operantis, et modum ipsius operationis; seu talis est modus, quo fit operatio, qualis est operantis natura. . ."—Signoriello, *Lexicon Peripateticum Philosophico-Theologicum* (5. ed., Romae: Pustet, 1931), p. 237.

[3] "Iurisdictio episcopalis, etsi possit per ius pontificium plus minusve restringi, semper tamen est de natura sua completa, ad omnes partes regiminis ecclesiastici in foro tam externo quam interno se extendens."—Billot, *Tractatus de Ecclesia Christi*, I, 711.

nature legislative, judicial and executive.[4] Canon 335, therefore, as in the other principles which it sets forth, so in its listing of the functional properties of episcopal jurisdiction, merely materially repeats the divinely constituted law *(ius divinum Ecclesiam constituens)*, explicitly interpreting its essential implications, and does not present a law formally instituted by the Church herself *(ius ab Ecclesia constitutum)*.

The legislative is the principal function of jurisdictional power. The other two, the judicial and the executive, are consequences of it both as to the necessity of their existence and the properties of their operation. The legislative function is that by which the social authority discerns, proposes, designates and prescribes the means to the attainment of the social end. Its necessity, then, is that of means for an end. It is that by which laws as such are instituted. It extends to all those measures which are either absolutely requisite for the simple attainment of the end, or relatively necessary (useful) for the more perfect and efficient acquisition thereof.[5]

Whatever controversies have been waged by authors on the subject of the bishop's legislative capacity have been concerned not so much with the fact itself, which all admit as at least eminently befitting, opportune and even at times relatively necessary or expedient for the proper purpose of the episcopate, but rather with its ultimate basis or origin. In the light of the foregoing argument this function of the episcopate is based on intrinsic necessity. Any contrary opinion, as for instance that of Suarez, must be rejected. The view of Suarez is that the bishop's legislative function is of human (ecclesiastical) origin with a basis in the divine law.[6] His conclusion is based on three premises,

[4] "Potestas pascendi et regendi simpliciter dicta, potestas est quae omnes regiminis ecclesiastici partes complectitur, et non est solum ad ministrandum sacramenta, verum etiam ad leges ferendum, ad exercendum judicia, ad puniendum contumaces."—Billot, *Tractatus de Ecclesia Christi*, I, 712.

[5] "Ius proponendi obligatorio modo quae necessaria et utilia sunt ad finem societatis assequendum."—Ottaviani, *Institutiones Iuris Publici Ecclesiastici*, I. n. 42.

[6] "Dicendum igitur censeo, Episcopos habere potestatem legislativam in

namely, 1) that the bishop's office was instituted by Christ but that the actual power attaching to it was left entirely to the Church as to its substantial import, 2) that the power of the episcopate, therefore, derives from the Sovereign Pontiff not only as to the fact of its immediate tenure by the individual bishop (a point which is even yet controverted) but also as to the kind of authority itself, 3) and finally that as a result of these two tenets, the Pope can institute particular episcopates without legislative power.[7]

The first of these premises is untenable, as is evident from the essential concept of the episcopate contained in the apostolic succession. It ignores the fact that any purpose (and so the episcopal office) demands a proportionate power for its attainment, so that if the one is necessary the other must also be. As to the second contention, while it may be true in regard to the immediate origin of episcopal power in the individual, it does not, and indeed cannot stand in regard to the substantial kind of power which attaches to the episcopate, in view of the falsity of the earlier premise. The third assertion is true in a sense, but false in so far as it is an overstatement. It fails to distinguish between the particular episcopates which by divine command are essential to the organization of the Church and those which in this essential sense are supernumerary. As to the latter the Pope can indeed refuse legislative power, but by that very fact these particular offices cannot be substantially perfect as required in the former.

The whole view, therefore, is rejected as contrary to the traditional mind of the Church.[8] The traditional view, even if not

suis dioecesibus jure ordinario humano fundato aliquo modo in divino . . . quia potestas ferendi leges non est de ratione intrinseca muneris episcopalis secundum generalem rationem suam. . ."—*Tractatus de Legibus*, lib. 4, c. 4, nn. 2, 23.

[7] Cf. *Tractatus de Legibus*, lib. 4, c. 4, nn. 5, 18, 20, 23.

[8] "Etenim, quum Episcopi positi sint a Spiritu Sancto *regere Ecclesiam Dei*, iisque collata sit potestas solvendi et ligandi . . . nemo, *salva Fide*, potest jurisdictionem illis abjudicare suas oves legibus obstringendi, quibus obtemperare cogantur."—Benedict XIV, *De Synodo Dioecesana*, lib. 13, c. 4, n. 3; Soglia, *Institutiones Iuris Publici Ecclesiastici*, lib. II, n. 52.

consciously or expressly based on the above argument relative to the fact that the episcopal power must be functionally integral is nevertheless aptly and sufficiently explained and justified thereby. It is required, first of all, that the episcopal power be endowed with a legislative function, since this is the prime manifestation of complete jurisdiction, from which the other functions take their origin and by the limits of which they are both extensively and intensively determined.

The *judicial* function is a necessary consequence of the legislative. Liwe the latter which postulates it, this function of jurisdiction has always been factually recognized in the episcopal power. Unless the intrinsic necessity of his legislative function is recognized, however, the judicial activity of the residential bishop cannot juridically be adequately vindicated. Given the laws as constituted, doubts and conflicts will inevitably arise regarding both their interpretation and their application. The purpose of the judicial function, therefore, is to interpret the meaning of the already existent law for concrete cases, declaring which acts or beliefs conform to or contradict the law, and what juridical consequences follow from such acts.[9]

Since it is a necessary practical consequence of his legislative right, the bishop whose power is substantially complete must also be capable of a proportionate judicial activity. That is, he must be able authoritatively to interpret and interpretatively to apply the law, declaring its significance in particular instances in order that the law as intended may obtain, and the social order which it effects may be preserved from violation or restored if already violated.[10]

An executive function must also be vindicated to the bishop's power as intrinsically requisite for its perfectly effective exercise. It is a necessary consequence of both the legislative and the judicial. It is also marked to some extent with the properties of both so as

[9] "Ius declarandi seu proponendi obligatorio modo, quaenam subditorum actiones in concreto sint iuri conformes, quaeque eidem difformes, et effectus legitimos eiusdem conformitatis aut difformitatis." —Cavagnis, *Institutiones Iuris Publici Ecclesiastici,* I, n. 115.

[10] Cf. Ottaviani, *Institutiones Iuris Publici Ecclesiastici,* I, n. 48.

to be a sort of extension of them. Given the provision of laws by legislative enactment and their interpretative application by judicial sentence, the executive function provides for the actual and immediate application of both.[11] If the bishop can make laws intended for general diocesan application, and can interpret them as they are intended for particular application, he must, unless his power is rather speculative than practical, be able also to effect that the law does actually in every instance apply both generally and particularly as intended. Unless the other two functions result in this third, they are juridically sterile. Moreover, this executive function itself would all too frequently be barren of efficacy in the application of the law unless it were possessed of the peculiar force which is explicitly attributed to this function of episcopal power by the use of the word *coactive* in the present canon. The effective application of the law demands the cooperation of its subjects. This cooperation, it is presumed, will for the most part be willingly extended. However, since it is an absolute requisite in the pursuit of the social end, it must be securable even from the unwilling. There are, therefore, two specific aspects of executive activity, the free and the forceful.

Although the term *executive* does not appear in the canonical delineation of the bishop's jurisdictional functions, its generic import is nevertheless amply insinuated and implied in the word *coactive.* This latter term, since it is employed in correlation to the terms legislative and judicial to denote a third function of the episcopal power, must be understood as denoting the extreme [12] and not the exclusive characteristic of the executive function. It is used not to eliminate any notion of a non-coercive function, for *qui potest maius potest et minus,* but rather to emphasize, in answer to both positive denial [13] and possible doubt, a characteristic of

[11] "Ius urgendi legum sententiarumque applicationem, dirigendo personas vel disponendo de rebus, atque removendo omnia obstacula quae finis socialis plenam assecutionem impediunt."—Ottaviani, *Institutiones Iuris Publici Ecclesiastici,* I, n. 56.

[12] "Ius *vim physicam* adhibendi in personas, ad finis socialis consecutionem."—Ottaviani, *Institutiones Iuris Publici Ecclesiastici,* I, n. 59.

[13] Cf. Ottaviani, *Institutiones Iuris Publici Ecclesiastici,* I. n. 41.

ecclesiastical power[14] in which the bishop shares. Moreover, since this coactive quality perfects his executive function itself, and since this perfect executive function in turn perfects as well as follows upon the other functions, the term coactive indicates also the positive intensity of the bishop's entire functional activity.

The substantial faculties of episcopal jurisdiction, together with the juridical matter on which these faculties may act and the modes or functions by which this essential operation applies to its object, having been discussed there remains, as the final topic of this treatise, a consideration of the juridical efficacy or force which attaches to the union of the episcopal right and object of jurisdiction.

Article II
Positive Intensity of Episcopal Jurisdiction

Although the terms legislative, judicial and coactive properly denote merely external manifestations of jurisdictional faculties applied and applying to their due object, the faculties themselves are so actively identified with their functions that the jurisdictional power itself is generally specified by these terms. It is, indeed, exclusively under these three aspects that social authority appears in practice, and according to the one or the other of them that it is exercised in concrete instances.[15] Consequently, the juridical intensity of the bishop's doctrinal and disciplinary faculties respectively will be discussed herein with reference to these three functional characteristics.

I. Doctrinal Force.

As was stated above in reference to the bishop's doctrinal office, he is the authoritative teacher of Christian doctrine in his diocese. His teaching is therefore authentic, which means that

[14] Cf. Denzinger-Bannwart, *Enchiridion,* nn. 1504, 1697, 1724.

[15] "Sicut anima humana, in se simplicissima, varias habet facultates inter se distinctas, quibus suam virtutem exercet, ita potestas gubernativa, quae in se nihil aliud est quam complexus jurium, hunc complexum resolvit essentialiter et ex natura rei in triplicem potestatem, dum operatur, aut proxime disposita ad operandum spectatur." —Grandeclaude, *Ius Canonicum* (3 vols., Parisiis, 1882), I, 107.

it is occasioned and sanctioned by a divine mission and has the force of exacting the assent of those whom he teaches.[16] However, his *individually* exercised doctrinal right has not the same force as that of the Pope alone, or of the universal episcopate in the ordinary or extraordinary magisterium of the Church.[17] Although the purpose of the essentially one ecclesiastical magisterium is to propagate the gospel of Christ, the individual officers to whom it is entrusted are not of equal competence. For though the deposit of faith itself is substantially perfect and cannot be increased by the Church, there are nevertheless in the Church various degrees of authoritatively teaching its contents and consequences, namely, the pontifical and the episcopal.

The former and highest degree is complete and independent, and has both infallible and universal force. It entails a legislative power, that is, a force sufficient to institute doctrine formally as such, affecting the innermost convictions of the mind. It alone can render the final judicial decisions in controversies concerning matters of doctrine. It alone, finally, can dispense this doctrine throughout the universal Church, and dispose with sovereign executive force the ways and means by which all other teachers are to fulfill their office of spreading the doctrine of Christ.[18]

The authority to teach which is attached to the office of the individual residential bishops has not the attributes of universality or infallibility. It is, therefore, partial and subordinate. It is *partial* because it is possessed of no formally legislative force as

[16] Cf. Egger, *Enchiridon Theologiae Dogmaticae Generalis* (6. ed., Brixinae: Typis et Sumptibus Wegerianis, 1932), n. 169.

[17] Since it is the *monarchic* tenure of episcopal jurisdiction which is considered in this treatise, we abstract from the import of the doctrinal position which the bishop, even though isolated in his diocese, holds in the collective episcopate. "Ut ordo episcopalis sua collegii apostolici missione et successione utatur, sufficit ut intendat pro suo munere magisterii collectivi docere, non autem requiritur ut localiter congregetur. Unitas enim publica magisterii constituitur, non communi praesentia in eodem loco, sed mentium et voluntatum concordia extrinsecus manifesta." —d'Herbigny, *Theologica de Ecclesia* (3. ed., 2 vols., Parisiis: Beauchesne, 1928), II, 393.

[18] Wilhelm-Scannell, *A Manual of Catholic Theology,* I, 35.

such, although it does shares to a degree in the judicial and executive functions of the ecclesiastical magisterium. The bishop, therefore, cannot in matters of faith make doctrinal laws for his respective diocese. He is placed over only a portion of the Church and his power is specifically diocesan; doctrinal truth, on the other hand, is universal, and a law requiring assent to a truth of this kind cannot be more restricted than truth itself, nor, as might practically result if individual bishops could legislate, can it substantially differ in the various sections of the Church. In short, although the individual bishop is the divinely appointed and therefore the pre-eminent *witness* and doctor of the faith in his diocese, his testimony of the truth is concerned with the already formally established doctrine. In this regard, moreover, although the individual bishop is not infallible even in his presentation and interpretation of the established doctrine, his position postulates the presumption that he is fully cognizant of and conversant with it. This presumption, in turn, requires at least a *provisional* and *practical* religious assent to his teaching on the part of those whom he instructs.[19] This acceptance of episcopal pronouncements in doctrinal matters is obligatory on his subjects to the extent that unless based on truly conscientious reasons a refusal of acceptance would brand one as temerarious and lacking in the respect and reverence due to divinely constituted authority. The bishop's pronouncements, it was said, demand a provisional assent. That is, they are to be considered authentic until the supreme voice of the Roman Pontiff states otherwise, unless they are patently erroneous. The bishop's

[19] "*Decretis Ecclesiae authenticis non infallibilius praestandus est assensus religiosus, quamvis non super omnia firmus.* Decreta haec non merentur assensum super omnia firmum, quippe cum eorum veritas non absolute constet; expostulant tamen assensum religiosum, quia procedunt a magisterio per Christum instituto et Christi auctoritate insignito. Assensus his decretis adhibendus duo complectitur: *silentium obsequiosum* sive *subiectionem externam,* quae postulat, ut locutione, scriptione aliisque actionibus externis contra decreta lata abstineatur; necnon *mentis obsequium* sive *subiectionem internam,* qua doctrinae talibus decretis propositae habeantur ut practice tutae et sequendae."—Felder, *Apologetica,* pp. 270-271.

teaching requires practical assent also. In other words it must be considered as expressing the mind of the Church and its implications and consequences must be a guiding influence in external behaviour.

The individual bishop's doctrinal authority is not only partial as to its jurisdictional intensity, but whatever juridical force it has is *subordinate.* While it has both a judicial and an executive function, neither of these is sovereign. Only the Chief Shepherd of the flock, the Pope, is the supreme promulgator of doctrine, the universal judge in matters of faith, the arbiter in controversies of faith and the father and teacher of all Christians. Although the bishop is competent in reference to a judicial and an executive function in doctrinal matters, neither of these has the force of finality, for his judicial power is not infallible nor is his executive power independent.

However, though the bishop cannot make a law of faith as such, he is nevertheless within certain limits a true judge of the faith. Just as it is his to present the true doctrine, so it is his to decide in particular instances what doctrines, theological or philosophical, are in conformity with revealed truth. He does not thereby effect a formal doctrinal decision, which declares a particular tenet to be contained in the deposit of faith. For just as the bishop has no formal legislative power in doctrinal matters because he is neither an infallible nor a universal authority, so his judicial decisions, which by the nature of his power are of purely diocesan import, cannot be formally constitutive of truth which cannot be territorially restricted and must procede from an infallible source. The bishop, then, merely states whether or not a doctrine is contrary to or compatible with the content of revelation either as defined or traditionally interpreted by the Church. His judicial function is directed to the defense of the faith by declaring a particular doctrine and its authors as heretical and, if necessary by imposing a proportionate penalty upon the latter.[20]

[20] "Relate ad causas fidei, Episcopus est *inquisitor natus et judex* non quidem ad ferendum judicium doctrinale de aliqua propositione (haec

The judgment of the bishop, therefore, has but the force of a judicial sentence which, pending an appeal, obligatorily affects directly only the parties involved, though indirectly the bishop's decision in such matters must also be considered a norm for the guidance of others in his diocese.[21]

Since he is concerned with the established doctrine as such, it is not the bishop's judicial prerogative to decide the legitimate controversies concerning the faith, or to solve doubts which are still tolerated in the Church.[22] In matters whether speculative or practical concerning which approved authors dispute, the bishop must officially be impartial.[23] He may not allow or prescribe only one side of a moralists' difference of opinion, but should see to it that a *via media* is proposed, one which is neither lax nor too rigorous,[24] and in questions about which there exists a doctrinal controversy among theologians, the solution of which has a directly practical reference, the bishop will prudently indicate as the present practical norm for his subjects no more than the Church officially prescribes in her common law.[25] If a doctrinal dispute of this latter sort, namely, one which has an immediate practical import,

est causa maior et Papae reservata), sed ad inquirendum utrum quis doctrinas haereticas sustinuerit, et ad ipsum judicandum."—Rivet, *Institutiones Iuris Ecclesiastici Privati*, p. 382.

21 "Nemo dubitat quin ad Episcopos potissimum pertineat, in haereticos inquirere, atque in illos, quos in suis erroribus pertinaces compererit, canonicis poenis severe animadvertere."—Benedict XIV, *De Synodo Dioecesana,* lib. 9, c. 4, n. 3.

22 "Aliquae sunt doctrinae palam haereticae apud omnes, aliae dubiae simplicibus, sed manifestae sapientibus et peritis; tertiae veluti neutrae, habentes pro se doctores cum rationibus in utramque partem probabilibus, nec in una tantum dioecesi, vel paucis, sed apud omnes Christianos, aut longe plurimos. Est vero veritas quod in primis et secundis *auctoritas inferiorum praelatorum* se extendit, et in suos tantummodo, in tertiis vero nequaquam, quoniam dicuntur maiores causae fidei, propter difficultatem decisionis cum periculo scandali; ideo sunt ad Sedem Ecclesiae, vel ad sedentem in ea referendae."—Gerson, *Tractatus de examinatione doctrinarum,* consideratio 3 — (*Opera Omnia,* 5 vols., Antverpiae, 1706), I, 10.

23 Benedict XIV, *De Synodo Dioecesana,* lib. 7, c. 15, n. 7.

24 Benedict XIV, *De Synodo Dioecesana,* libe. 12, c. 6, n. 12.

25 Benedict XIV, *De Synodo Dioecesana,* lib. 7, c. 16, n. 13.

hinges *entirely* on the theological interpretations of the practical common law as evidencing the doctrinal mind of the Church, the bishop can inject himself somewhat into the controversy by prohibiting, if he deems it necessary for the particular needs of his diocese, what many may claim to be permitted by the law at issue.[26] In thus deciding according to one side of a dispute, the bishop does not exactly render a judicial decision as such, but rather interprets the common law, within its possible scope, in accordance with what he deems to be the best practical application of that law for his diocese. He functions rather executively than judicially. This leads to the consideration of the bishop's executive force in doctrinal matters.

The executive is the most forceful function of the bishop's doctrinal faculty. The purpose of his judicial function in matters of faith is the defense of the truth against particular abuses, whether they be actual or at least seemingly so. The purpose of his executive function is the general preservation and dissemination of the faith througout his diocese. His judicial activity is also ultimately directed to this end, but in the compartively negative way of repelling actual attack rather than in the positive manner evidenced in the executive acts. These executive acts are ordained to the prevention of error and the propagation of the faith, the former directly by means of the latter.

The executive use of the bishop's magisterial power cannot be entirely separated from his disciplinary activity, since the prime purpose of the latter is to regulate the practical life of his subjects in accordance with their beliefs. The disciplinary authority of the episcopate is ultimately intended as a means to the proper practice of the Christian faith. It is, therefore, inseparable from

[26] "Accidit interdum rem aliquam in questionem adduci nondum ab Ecclesia difinitam, et nihilominus integrum esse Episcopo aliquid de illa decernere, citra violationem regulae . . . etenim, aliquando totius controversiae cardo unice vertitur circa ius commune, quo solum inspecto, disputant Theologi, utrum aliquid fieri liceat, necne; ceterum nullus eorum abjudicat Episcopo potestatem, illud suo peculari statuto inhibendi, quod plerique contendunt esse a jure communi permissum."—Benedict XIV, *De Synodo Dioecesana,* lib. 7, c. 3, n. 1.

the complete prosecution of the bishop's doctrinal purpose. There is, however, a purely doctrinal aspect to the episcopal activity in matters of the faith, and although it may be complete in itself it is relatively imperfect. This is the actual ***instruction*** of the faithful in religious and moral matters, whether it be given orally or in writing, personally or through others.[27]

Since it is for the bishop to spread and to intensify the faith by prevention of error as well as by the presentation of the truth, and since the object of his doctrinal authority comprises both spiritual and temporal truths related thereto, he will not only provide sufficient explanation of the Church's teaching, but will see to it that contrary doctrines are brought to the attention of his flock in order that they may be warned of the danger, lest they unwarily become victims of its too often enticing aspects.[28]

In presenting the norm of Christian truth the bishop will necessarily at times touch upon secular questions which bear upon religion and morality. This is his prerogative, and his interpretation in such cases is just as authoriative as is his teaching on purely religious and moral subjects. Moreover, since there may often be a certain amount of obscurity in such matters of a mixed nature, not only is the bishop in his diocese and for his diocese to teach authoritatively within the limits of faith and morals, but it is also for him to decide and declare authoritatively in cases of doubt how far these limits extend. Though in these questions opinion may be divided, or the bishop's authority to pronounce may at least be the more readily doubted or denied, since it is all but impossible to give a hard and fast rule as to

[27] "Episcopi singuli magisterium suum exercent tum viva voce tum litteris scriptis. *Viva voce,* dum episcopi sive ipsi sive per presbyteros in concionibus aliisque instructionibus populum docent. *Litteris scriptis* episcopi docent dum 'mandata' aliasve epistulas fidelibus publice communicandas mittunt."—Felder, *Apologetica,* (2. ed., Paderbornae: Schoeningh, 1923).

[28] "Quamvis enim nequeat Episcopus quaestiones definire ad Fidei doctrinam pertinentes, non tamen prohibetur, ne aut in Synodo aut extra Synodum, *cavendos jubeat errores,* iam ab Ecclesia proscriptos." —Benedict XIV, *De Synodo Dioecesana,* lib. 6, c. 3, n. 7.

where the bishop's doctrinal jurisdiction ends in such matters, it is the bishop himself and he alone who is competent to determine the limits of his power. This decision is, of course, subject to appeal, but meanwhile it stands, just as the teaching itself stands, as the supreme diocesan magisterial pronouncement.

The foregoing applies to the bishop's teaching when it is official. His views, on whatever topic, as privately presented, that is, spoken or written by him in his capacity as a private person, have no more juridical force than is warranted by the basis on which they rest, and without sufficient rational and authoritative foundation the bishop himself will refrain from introducing his purely private views into his government of the diocese.

The actual manner in which the official instruction for which he is competent is to be given, the means by which it is to be provided, the regulation of external acts consequent to it, all these pertain, indeed, to the bishop's doctrinal office. However, the functions themselves involved in this enforcement of his teaching are not purely doctrinal, but imply and involve the exercise of the episcopal disciplinary faculty.

II. Disciplinary Force.

Since the practice of the faith is its fundamental purpose, the whole disciplinary activity of the residential bishop may properly be considered as ordained to the executive fulfillment of his doctrinal office. In the use of his disciplinary faculty to this end the bishop may function with legislative, judicial and executive force. His disciplinary concern is the whole practical life of his subjects in matters of religious significance. He is materially limited in scope only as the quantitative object of his jurisdiction was above described as limited, namely, his jurisdiction is specifically diocesan, which ultimately signifies that only those things are positively excluded from the sphere of his power which are contrary to the higher law, whether common or particular. The disciplinary activity of the bishop, therefore, may be either in accord with (*secundum ius*) or beyond the higher law (*praeter ius),* divine or ecclesiastical.[29]

[29] "Pleno iure exercet Episcopus *imperium* in personas et res eccles-

1. Legislative Function.

Legislatively, therefore, the bishop may function both according to and beyond the higher law. His legislation *secundum ius* is directed to the adaptation of the higher law to his diocese. The higher law is the superior legislator's mind as to the means of procuring a particular end. In accomodating the higher law to the specific territorial characteristics of his diocese, the bishop must take cognizance of both the mind of the superior legislator and the purpose which the superior legislator intends, since both of these must be substantially respected and preserved intact. The bishop's legislation *secundum ius* consists in specifically determining according to the pecularities of his diocese those matters which the higher law merely generically regulates without further remark as to their particular application, or which are explicitly left to the bishop by the superior legislator for more accurate regulation. The bishop thus, as it were, perfects the higher law. He specifies its particular import for his diocese, and this is the precise role for which his potential capability, described above as specifically diocesan, is intended in the legislative hierarchy as regards the higher law.

In specifying the higher law for his diocese, the bishop may in virtue of his legislative function *secundum ius,* unless the superior legislator has expressly ruled otherwise, institute sanctions for the higher law. He may, if the higher law itself carries no sanctiion, or if the law while providing for sanctions expressly leaves the determination of the same to the bishop, strengthen the significance of the law in his diocese by prescribing particular penalties for its violation.[30] He may also add his own sanction to that which the higher law already carries unless the superior

iasticas suae dioecesis, quas, tum legis universalis applicatione, tum dioecesanis statutis, tum particulari praecepto, valet ad debitum finem supernaturalem dirigere."—Deshayes, *Memento Iuris Ecclesiastici,* n. 641.

[30] "Exploratum hodie apud omnes est potestatem legislativam Episcoporum pertinere ut legibus suis quasi perficiant quod ius commune relinquerit minus definitum et sancitum, ita ut nihil ab ipsis contra ius commune vel eius directionem statui possit."—S.C.C., 19 feb. 1921—*AAS,* XIII (1921), 228; cf. e.g., canons 2220 § 1, 2221.

legislator has ruled otherwise.[31] In this last case, however, and especially if the higher law as it stands is sanctioned by a milder penalty than in the past, there must be proportionately grave causes warranting the further and possibly more severe and intensive sanction as regards the bishop's diocese.[32]

Given the regulation of a particular matter by the higher law, the bishop acting in accordance with it not only cannot prescribe what is opposed thereto,[33] or permit what is prohibited thereby, but neither can he prohibit what is *explicitly* permitted therein, unless the law itself or the superior legislator concedes him this right.[34] He may, however, prohibit what is doubtfully or only implicitly permitted,[35] although he may not permit what is even merely implicitly prohibited by the higher law.

Episcopal legislation *praeter ius* is directed toward supplying the defects of other legislation in view of the specifically diocesan needs.[36] The matters embraced by this species of episcopal legis-

[31] "Etenim nihil magis est apud Doctores receptum, quam quod Episcopus queat Jus Commune adjuvare, poenasque augere ab illo inflictas."—Benedict XIV, *De Synodo Dioecesana,* lib. 10, c. 11, n. 4; cf. e.g., canon 2247, § 1.

[32] Benedict XIV, *De Synodo Dioecesana,* lib. 10, c. 11, n. 4; cf. e.g., canon *Commentarium pro Religiosis.* v. I (1920), 370.

[33] "Nihil magis vulgatum est, quam quod Synodalis constitutio contra Jus Commune et Apostolicas sanctiones, nullius sit roboris et firmitatis." —Benedict XIV, *De Synodo Dioecesana,* lib. 12, c. 1, n. 1.

[34] "Notandum est episcopos et generales auctores legum particularium nihil statuere posse contra ius commune aut decreta Concilii plenarii aut provincialis; unde, nisi lex superior id disserte concedat, nec prohibere possunt quod iure communi *expresse* [i.e., *explicite*], permittitur, nec permittere quod iure communi prohibetur. . ."—Tanquerey, *Synopsis Theologiae Moralis et Pastoralis* (8. ed., 3 vols., Parisiis: Desclee, 1927), II, n. 285.

[35] Cf. Genicot-Salsman, *Institutiones Theologiae Moralis* (12. ed., 2 vols., Bruxelles: Dewit, 1931), I, n. 96; cf. Wernz, *Ius Decretalium,* II, n. 756 quoted by the S. C. C., 19 feb. 1921,—*AAS,* XIII (1921), 228: "Inde quoque sequitur episcopus suis legibus nihil posse prohibere quod iure communi expresse *et indubitanter est permissum. . ."* This obviously does not refer to what is express but merely implicit.

[36] "Dum Episcopi potestate non pollent condendi leges aut decreta contra ius, scilicet, contra generales Ecclesiae leges, ipsi *plena* potestate

lation are, as has been said, the particular concern of the residential episcopate as a juridic entity distinct from the papacy. They are, consequently, those in which the bishop's power is both more extensive and more intensive than in any others.[37] They include whatever is not opposed to the higher law in the sense that although it is neither implicitly nor explicitly contained in the higher law, it is nevertheless entirely compatible with the content of that law, and at the same time requires no higher authority for its regulation. Episcopal legislation *praeter ius* is also directed to the supplying of those needs which have not been consulted by previous diocesan legislation. Such previous diocesan legislation, established either by his predecessors in office or himself, will be either in accordance with or beyond the higher law. Since such particular legislation originates in the same source and stands in virtue of the same power which he now holds, the bishop may not only legislate further according to the existent diocesan law, or beyond it, but he may also go contrary to it, thereby abrogating the previous particular law, without, however, contravening the superior law now in force.

In his legislation both according to and beyond the higher law, the bishop must recognize and respect a universal custom which has acquired the force of common law.[38] However, although he cannot of himself introduce any change in the higher law, he may authentically declare that a legitimate custom has been introduced in his diocese against the higher law,[39] without, however, incorporating such a custom into a positive statute, since

praediti sunt condendi leges ac decreta praeter ius, scilicet, quae iuri communi non adversentur."—Signatura Apostolica, 15 dec. 1923—*AAS*, XVI (1924), 107.

[37] "Ob hanc potestatem licet Episcopis per leges ac decreta ea omnia statuere, quae ipsi in dioecesis regimine opportuniora censeant."—Signatura Apostolica, 15 dec. 1923—*AAS*, XVI (1924), 106.

[38] Benedict XIV, *De Synodo Dioecesana*, lib. 14, c. 2, n. 14.

[39] "Neminem enim latet quod in lege generali Ecclesiae nequeunt episcopi, vel in synodo vel extra synodum, aliquam mutationem inducere, valent tamen declarare authentice consuetudinem esse inductam adversus ius commune eamque firmare."—S R. R., 18 iul. 1914—*AAS*, VI (1914), 556-557.

this would be equivalent to his going positively and directly contrary to the higher law,[40] unless the superior legislator authorizes such action.

Episcopal laws have *per se* all the characteristics of particular positive law. They must conform to all the natural conditions common to all such laws, and also *per se* to these common requirements only. There are no peculiarly proper conditions, such as confirmation by the higher authority, for instance,[41] demanded by the nature of episcopal authority in order that the bishop's laws (within the legitimate scope of the bishop's potential and actual capacity) may have the full force or include the various species of law, although the Roman Pontiff may obviously establish such conditions and restrict both the intensity and the extent of episcopal legislation, as long as the bishop retains truly legislative power.[42]

There is, therefore, no natural objective basis for the distinction which many authors [43] have made in the past, namely, that Synodal decrees are truly laws, but that extra-synodal decrees, (unless they affect all diocesans or the bishop clearly signifies his intention of instituting a law) are merely precepts.[44] Moreover, unless there is a positive regulation to this effect made by the higher authority, or the manifest intention of the bishop himself, there can be no basis whatever for such a distinction. Nor con-

[40] Benedict XIV, *De Synodo Dioecesana,* lib. 12, c. 8, n. 8, 12.

[41] Benedict XIV, *De Synodo Dioecesana,* lib. 13, c. 3, n. 6.

[42] "Legisferam potestatem Episcopis, quamdiu Episcopi manent, S. Pontifex adimere nequit, utcunque tota jurisdictionis potestas Episcopis a S. Pontifice communicatur. Juris enim divini est ut Episcopus, quamdiu Episcopus est, habeat potestatem, quae ad dioecesis gubernationem necessaria sit. Potest vero S. Pontifex pro circumstantiis temporum et locorum certas res sibi reservare, potest certas leges Episcopi abolere, potest certam normam certasque conditiones praescribere, quae ad licitum et ad validum legisferae potestatis exercitium pertineant."—Lehmkuhl, *Theologia Moralis* (6. ed., 2 vols., Friburgi Brisgoviae, 1890), I, n. 122.

[43] Cf. e.g., Tanquerey, *Synopsis Theologiae Moralis et Pastoralis* (8. ed., 3 vols., Parisiis: Desclee, 1927), II, n. 285; Lehmkuhl, *Theologia Moralis* (6. ed., 2 vols., Friburgi Brisgoviae, 1890), I, n. 122.

[44] Wernz, *Ius Decretalium,* I, n. 182.

sequently is there any natural foundation for the further distinction derived by many authors, namely, that since extra-synodal decrees are precepts rather than laws they are not perpetual and that only Synodal legislation perdures in force after the death, physical or juridical, of the legislator.

The bishop's power legislatively and otherwise is radically monarchic and *per se* immediate, so that—given no positive regulation to the contrary—he need not in legislating consult, seek the advice or have the consent of any other diocesan authority or obtain the confirmation of the higher authority.[45] The position of other diocesan officials is that of participants in the bishop's naturally and radically undiminished monarchic authority. Any directly collaborative part which they play in diocesan government adds nothing essential to the monarchic prerogative of the bishop. It is at most merely a *conditio sine qua non* established by the higher authority as an aid to the bishop, either in those matters which he is personally unable to manage alone or in which the advice, help and judgment of others may be practically necessary or conducive to more efficient and prudent regulation. The Sovereign Pontiff may make such rules regarding the difference between episcopal laws and precepts and their respective duration. The bishop himself may intend to act according to such a norm. The Pope, however, must do so by positive act, and the intention of the bishop, so long as there is no such positive decree by the supreme authority, may not be presumed as in accord with this distinction, but must rather be clearly proven since the presumption is to the contrary.[46] It is only when there is a really substantiated doubt that the rule might in practice be followed that synodal decrees would be regarded as laws and perpetual, and extrasynodal decrees would be considered as percepts and temporary.[47] The same applies to all similar conditions and restrictions of the bishop's legislative prerogative, since such are not founded

[45] Cf. canons 335 § 2 and 362.

[46] Cf. Benedict XIV, *De Synodo Dioecesana,* lib. 13, c. 5, n. 1.

[47] Cf. Chelodi, *Ius de Personis* (Tridenti: Libr. edit. Tridentini, 1922), p. 287; Rivet, *Institutiones Iuris Ecclesiastici Privati,* I, 381.

in the nature of episcopal legislation, but only on the will of the bishop himself or the intention of the Roman Pontiff.

Episcopal legislation, moreover, may *per se* be of any and all species: prescriptive, permissive, prohibitive, territorial, personal, penal, and even the so-called invalidating and inhabilitating laws, so long as no positive restriction has been placed upon the bishop's natural competency in this regard.[48] Thus, the bishop's laws may be intended as *simply* territorial and therefore binding only his domiciliary or quasi-domiciliary subjects, and these only when they are actually present in the diocese. This is the usual and presumed intention of the bishop, in accord with the recognized principle as to the natural territoriality of law.[49] They may, however, on the other hand, be intended as absolutely territorial and binding all who are physically present in the diocese, whether they be regular inhabitants thereof, transients *(peregrini)* or vagrants *(vagi)*.[50] Episcopal laws may likewise be personal and binding only a particular class of persons, clerical or lay, permanent or temporary subjects of the bishop. Thus, the bishop may establish laws for *peregrini* and *vagi* only, or for his ordinary subjects only, in accord, however, with the principles enunciated in the discussion concerning the personal object of episcopal jurisdiction, namely, that while *vagi* are subject to the bishop to the *maximum* necessary extent, *peregrini* are subject to him only to the *minimum* necessary extent.

With regard to invalidating laws, the bishop cannot prescribe conditions for the validity of any matter which the Holy See has regulated without such invalidating provision,[51] unless this power is conceded to him by the supreme legislator, since such

[48] Chelodi, *Ius de Personis*, p. 287; Rivet, *Institutiones Iuris Ecclesiastici Privati*, I, 17; Wernz, *Ius* Decretalium, I, 93-94; Torrubiano Ripoll, *Novisimas instituciones de derecho canonico* (2. ed., Madrid, 1934), I, 88; Maroto, *Institutiones iuris canonici ad normam Codicis* (3. ed., 3 vols., Matriti, 1918), I 186; Cappello, *Summa Iuris Canonici*, I, 377.

[49] Canon 8 § 2; 13 § 2; Benedict XIV, *De Synodo Dioecesana*, lib. 13, c .4, n. 3.

[50] Cf. Van Hove, *De Legibus Ecclesiasticis*, n. 125.

[51] Benedict XIV, *De Synodo Dioecesana*, lib. 9, c. 1, n. 8.

a procedure would be tantamount to prohibiting what is explicitly permitted by the higher law. In the matter of attaching sanctions to his laws the bishop can decree penalties of any sort for which the Church as a whole is competent.[52] There should be a truly objective warrant and cause for such action, however, and the nature and intensity of the sanction should be tempered to the gravity of the matter at issue, with consideration of all the circumstances of person, place and time.[53] There is possible no general norm whereby the bishop may be guided in establishing sanctions.[54] It is left to his prudent judgment to decide the advisability of penalties, in accordance with the traditionally merciful mind and practice of the Church,[55] as well as in view of whatever positive regulations may exist on the subject at issue.

[52] Canon 2216.

[53] Benedict XIV, *De Synodo Dioecesana,* lib. 10, c. 1, n. 3. Benedict XIV states that the bishop should consider the number and frequency of the offenses which he penalizes, lest in decreeing general sanctions because of a few infractions by those of a certain class, the whole class be suspect and to the scandal of the faithful at large; cf. lib. 11, c. 4, n. 7; although he notices that circumstances may render grave a matter which is of itself of relatively minor importance, that is, in view of the danger of abuse whereby the example of a few may lead to a general disregard of the law; cf. lib. 10, c. 3.

[54] Benedict XIV, *De Synodo Dioecesana,* lib. 10, c. 3, n. 4.

[55] "Prae oculis autem habeatur monitum Conc. Trid., *sess.* XIII, *de ref.,* cap. 1: 'Meminerint Episcopi aliique Ordinarii se pastores non percussores esse, atque ita praeesse sibi subditos oportere, ut non in eis dominentur, sed illos tanquam filios et fratres diligant elaborentque ut hortando et monendo ab illicitis deterreant, ne, ubi deliquerint, debitis eos poenis coercere cogantur; quos tamen si quid per humanam fragilitatem peccare contigerit, illa Apostoli est ab eis servanda praeceptio ut illos arguant, obsecrent, increpent in omni bonitate et patientia, cum saepe plus erga corrigendos agat benevolentia quam austeritas, plus exhortatio quam comminatio, plus caritas quam potestas; sin autem ob delicti gravitatem virga opus erit, tunc mansuetudine rigor, cum misericordia iudicium, cum lenitate severitas adhibenda est, ut sine asperitate disciplina, populis salutaris ac necessaria, conservetur et qui correcti fuerint, emendentur aut, si resipiscere noluerint, ceteri, salubri in eos animadversionis exemplo, a vitiis deterreantur."—Canon 2214 § 2.

2. Judicial Function.

As to the judicial function of his disciplinary faculty, the residential bishop is by native right the proper ordinary judge of first instance [56] in all ecclesiastical causes [57] which by reason of any of the various recognized titles pertain to his diocese and are not reserved to the higher authority of the Roman Pontiff.[58] His judicial competence is proportionate to his legislative right, in the sense that he may function both according to and beyond the higher law. He judges according to the higher law all those matters which have been regulated by that law. He judges beyond the higher law all those matters which have been regulated by diocesan law, whether these diocesan laws themselves are according to or beyond the higher law. In judging according to the higher law the bishop does not authoritatively interpret that law, but rather interprets the facts in question with reference to the law as intended by the superior legislator. In judging beyond the higher law, the bishop not only estimates the facts of the question at issue in relation to the law of the diocese but also authoritatively and authentically interprets that law, since he himself is the legislator and consequenty the competent judge of his own mind in the matter. He is bound in any case to follow the prescribed rules of procedure established in the interests of justice. In all cases he authoritatively declares the juridical consequences which have been occasioned by particular violations of the law where such violations are found to have occured.

Although as the monarchic superior of the diocese the bishop himself may personally function in all judicial matters [59] which have not been withdrawn from the scope of his jurisdiction, it has almost become a principle of law that he should commit this function to others, especially in cases of criminal causes and others of grave importance. The reason which persuades such a

[56] Canon 1572 § 1.
[57] Canon 1553.
[58] Canons 1560-1568; 1557.
[59] Canon 1578.

relegation of judicial authority to others is that matters which require judicial procedure can safely and efficiently be conducted by others than the bishop himself, since the rules of procedure are substantially well-established and for the most part can be easily followed. It is, moreover, expedient that these matters be committed to others because they require so much time both as to the preparations and the formalities involved and would considerably impede the bishop in his attendance to other affairs of his office, some of which cannot be entrusted to others as judicial matters can, and most of which require his personal attention in that they depend not so much on definitely established norms as upon personal judgment and knowledge and must frequently be handled with more or less dispatch.[60] Finally, the nature and content of many judicial matters is such as to render the bishop's actual presence in person rather unfitting, since the matters discussed are not particularly consonant with the dignity of his position, especially those which concern criminal questions.[61]

3. Executive Function.

All other jurisdictional activity of the bishop, legislative and judicial culminates in and is perfected by his executive function. This is the ultimate stage of diocesan government to which all other functions, doctrinal and disciplinary, are directed, and without which the purpose of the bishop's power could not be attained. The executive force of the bishop's disciplinary faculty is, like the judicial, proportionate to his legislative prerogative. That is to say, the bishop's executive authority is directed to the immediate practical application of all the laws which are

[60] "Judices singulares in dioecesibus nativa potestate sunt Episcopi, qui tamen, negotiorum mole oppressi, aliis consueverunt committere causas judicandas."—Roberti, *De Processibus,* (2 vols., Romae: Apud Aedes Facultatis Iuridicae ad S. Apollinaris, 1929), I, n. 95.

[61] "Quia judicialis disceptatio, praecipue vero ea quae habetur in rebus gravioribus, quae in tribunalibus collegialibus tractantur, praeterquam multum temporis insumit, quo Episcopus indiget ad alia negotia quae non possunt alteri committi, non est apta conciliare Episcopo reverentiam ac fiduciam subditorum tantopere necessarias pro eorundem bono spirituali supernaturali."—Noval, *Commentarium Codicis Iuris Canonici,* Lib. IV, *De Processibus,* (Romae: Marietti, 1920), n. 127.

in force in his diocese, and consequently it may proceed both according to and beyond the higher law.

In executively acting according to the higher law the bishop applies and enforces that law both as instituted by the superior legislator for general diocesan application and as judicially applied to particular instances. In executively acting beyond the higher law the bishop applies and enforces the particular diocesan laws which either he himself or his precedessors in office have established according to and beyond the higher law.

In both cases much of the bishop's activity depends naturally on his own judgment and discretion, though obviously more personal latitude is possible in the application and enforcement of the diocesan laws than in that of the higher law. The superior legislator himself may have specified the norms to be followed in the application of the higher law. These, of course, the bishop must follow. On the other hand, since the laws which are purely episcopal regulate problems which the superior legislator has either not regulated at all or at most indefinitely, and since they are enacted by the bishop according to his own judgment of diocesan conditions, their application and enforcement must conform to those conditions in the concrete and consequently will depend to a much greater extent upon the bishop's own judgment. Thus, for example, the bishop can not in any way substantially dispense from the provisions of the higher law, except and in so far as this is permitted him by the superior legislator himself.[62] In regard to diocesan laws, however, just as he can altogether abrogate these laws so the bishop can dispense with their application when in his own judgment such relaxation of the law is more conducive to the spiritual welfare of his subjects.

It is all but impossible to enumerate the various executive activities of episcopal jurisdiction. The specific purpose of the bishop's office in this regard, however, may be distinguished according to its object as twofold: the authoritative direction of persons and the authoritative adminstration of material means or temporalities, both of which may be effected when necessary

[62] Canon 81.

by the use of physical force, spiritual or temporal coercion. The executive function of the bishop's authority entails the whole content of canonical legislation relative to both persons and property, by which the bishop must be guided in the conduct of his office.

Although as the monarchic superior of his diocese the bishop has the official power and competence to conduct all these diocesan affairs personally and alone, he is not personally able practically to do so because of their multiplicity. Others of the clergy are associated with him and share his authority in this regard. Their status and function is of ecclesiastical origin and is largely determined by the higher ecclesiastical law, since it is a matter of basic import and must be uniformly regulated throughout the Universal Church. Within the limits of the positive higher law, however, the bishop remains the supreme official of the diocese. As such, therefore, he authoritatively directs the clergy not only in their private lives as Christians, just as he does in regard to the laity, but in their official public lives as well, whether their official status concern the direction of person,[63] clerical or lay, or the administration of the diocesan temporalities.[64] Although by reason of the positive law the bishop may be neither the only nor the immediate director and administrator of diocesan affairs, he is nevertheless always the supreme official in every regard.[65] The unity of the Church which, as explained previously, demands the radically monarchic tenure of episcopal jurisdiction likewise demands that, no matter to what extent others may

[63] "Episcopus sacerdotes suos cogere potest, quoties necessitas bonumque publicum id exigat, si viribus polleant, ad sedulam navendam operam pro salute animarum."—S. C. C., 9 iul., 1881—*ASS*, XIV, 547

[64] "Sicut autem Episcopi ex ordinatione divina sunt qui praesunt Ecclesiae, ita ipsi non possunt ab eorundem bonorum cura, dispositione ac vigilantia excludi."—Pius VII, litt. apos. ad Epis. Amer. Septen., 24 aug. 1822—Coll. S. C. de Prop. Fide, I, n. 773; cf. also nn. 617, 712.

[65] Cf. Benedict XIV, *De Synodo Diocesana*, lib. 4, c. 4, n. 1; S. R. R., 28 feb. 1919—*AAS*, XII (1920), 90. Cf. Wernz, *Ius Decretalium*, III, nn. 150-151; Prümmer, *Manuale Iuris Canonici*, n. 449; Nebrada, "*Quaestiones selectae de Iure Administrativo Ecclesiastico*,"—*Commentarium pro Religiosis*, VII (1926), p. 261.

participate in the episcopal authority, the bishop himself as the radical source of that particpated power remain the supreme diocesan official. His position as such is necessary not only to procure and preserve doctrinal and disciplinary uniformity so far as possible, but also in order to obtain that *unity of spirit* which, as a constitutional feature of the Church, must characterize the relation of all the social members of the diocesan society: the relation of the clergy and the laity, and especially in regard to the former to effect the harmonious cooperation of the lesser clergy among themselves, and of their whole body, individually and collectively, with the bishop [66] in the execution of an office so difficult and exacting that it is all but impossible of perfect fulfillment.[67]

[66] "Ad hanc Ecclesiae constitutionem, quam nemo mortalium mutare potest, actio est accomodanda vitae. Propterea quemadmodum Episcopis necessaria est cum Apostolica Sede in gerendo episcopatu coniunctio, ita clericos laicosque oportet cum Episcopis suis coniunctissime vivere, agere."—Leo XIII, litt. encycl. *"Sapientiae christianae,"* 10 ian. 1890, n. 19—*Fontes,* n. 605.

[67] Episcoporum officium, quod oneris potius quam honoris loco pii homines semper habuerunt, adeo arduum est, ut vix ullus inter mortales reperiri queat, qui digne, id est, pefecte et absolute exsequatur. Laboriosissimum quippe est onus quodque ob innumera fere pericula et molestias vel Angelorum humeri ferre recusant."—Conc. Plen. Balt. II, tit. 3, c. 2, n. 84.

CONCLUSION

Principles are at once the most extensive and the most restrictive of truths. The practice which employs them is limited to their rigid extent, but within that area can travel a road whose labyrinthine possibilities allow that flexibility which times and occasions demand. The importance of principles cannot be overstressed. They are the measure of all that matters. Whenever authority is impugned, or even denied, a return to principles is the only solution, because ignorance or rejection of them is invariably the source of the struggle. The important point is that the change which their specific application in legitimate practice effects is a quantitative, not a qualitative, one.

While in the foregoing approach to the subject of episcopal jurisdiction there is to be found nothing substantially new, since the general concept is of faith, and attempt has been made to isolate the precisely juridical import of the episcopate and thus to present the particular canonical implications of the residential episcopate in so far as the subject pertains to the science of public ecclesiastical law.

As a divinely established constitutional feature of the Church's social organization, the residential episcopate has naturally and necessarily undergone no essential change or development. As long as practical acceptance was undisturbed, except for the dissent of relatively minor heretical and schismatic factions, one finds little authoritative exposition of episcopal jurisdiction, professedly as such. When later the institution and its corresponding power were attacked or abused, both the apologetic defense, in the one case, and the purely juridical implications, in the other, were approached in a rather close association with the concept of episcopal Orders. This was not only unnecessary but unfortunate. The purely historical question as to the origin of the unitary form of episcopal government became confused, and the canonical question as to the relation of pope and bishop remained obscure. In the one case, episcopal Orders were seen as generative of jurisdiction and necessarily supposing it. In the other, the equality of Orders in both bishop and pontiff led many to false conclusions as to their relative jurisdictional authority, since the sacrament of Orders was regarded as the basis of power in both.

The separate discussion herein followed is an attempt to clarify the issue in both instances. The historically evident correlation between episcopal Orders and episcopal jurisdiction does not warrant any conclusion as to their essential interpendence. Nor can the juridical nature of the lesser episcopate be adequately conceived without attention to the papal primacy which radically determines all other authority within the Church.

In discussing the jurisdictional status and function of the episcopate a distinction must be made between the particular episcopates which are essential and necessary in the Church by divine dispensation and those which are beyond this number whatsoever it may be, since the power of the Sovereign Pontiff is not absolute or unlimited as to the former. The jurisdictional authority of those bishops whose number is required by divine command must always be left substantially perfect in its sphere, and by comparison with the exclusive notes of the primatial jurisdiction of the Roman Pontiff it may be defined as specifically diocesan in its potential capability.

This potentiality, however, must be distinguished from its actualization or practical function. The former is determined by the nature of the office as established by Christ, whereas the latter is not so determined. It is left to the authority of the Pope to regulate the degree of actual realization of the bishop's potential power according to the demands of the Universal Church, within limits, however, which allow the bishop substantially perfect doctrinal and disciplinary faculties together with their necessary legislative, judicial and executive functions.

BIBLIOGRAPHY

Sources

Acta Apostolicae Sedis (AAS), Commentarium Officiale, Romae, 1909—

Acta Sanctae Sedis (ASS), 41 vols., Romae, 1865-1908.

Acta et Decretà Sacrorum Conciliorum Recentiorum, Collectio Lacensis, 7 vols., Friburgi Brisgoviae, 1870-1890.

Codex Iuris Canonici Pii X Pontificis Maximi iussu digestus, Benedicti Papae XV auctoritate promulgatus, Romae: Typis Polyglottis Vaticanis, 1917.

Codicis Iuris Canonici Fontes cura Emi. Petri Card. Gasparri editi, 8 vols., Romae, 1923-1938. (Vols. VII and VIII ed. cura et studio Emi Iustiniani Card. Serédi).

Denzinger, Henr. et Bannwart, Clem., *Enchiridion Symbolorum definitionum et declarationum de rebus fidei et morum,* 16. and 17. ed., Friburgi Brisgoviae: Herder, 1928.

Mansi, Joannes, *Sacrorum Conciliorum Nova et Amplissima Collectio,* 53 vols., Parisiis, 1901-1927.

Migne, Jacques, *Patrologiae Cursus Completus, Series Latina (MPL),* 221 vols., Parisiis, 1844-1864.

Migne, Jacques, *Patrologiae Cursus Completus, Series Graeca (MPG),* 161 vols., Parisiis, 1856 1866.

Pallottini, Salvator, *Collectio Omnium Conclusionum et Resolutionum quae in causis propositis apud S. Cong. Cardinalium S. Concilii Tridentini Interpretum prodierunt ab anno 1564 ad annum 1860,* 17 vols., Romae, 1868-1893.

Pius VI, *Responsio super Nunciaturis,* Romae, 1789; Florentiae, 1790.

Authors

Andreucci, *Hierarchia ecclesiastica in varias suas partes distributa,* Romae, 1766.

Antonelli, *De regimine ecclesiae episcopalis,* Venetiis, 1705.

Aristotle, *Politica,* Berlin: Reimer, 1831-1870.

[Bachofen], Charles Augustine, *A Commentary on the New Code of Canon Law,* 4. ed., 8 vols., St. Louis: B. Herder, 1921-1925.

Rights and Duties of Ordinaries, St. Louis: B. Herder, 1924.

Bachofen, Augustinus, *Summa Iuris Ecclesiastici Publici,* Romae: Puste, 1910

Barbosa, Augustinus, *Pastoralis sollicitudinis sive de officio et potestate Episcopi tripartita descriptio,* Lugduni, 1656.

Batiffol, Pierre, *Études d'histoire et de théologie positive,* Paris, 1907.

——— *Primitive Catholicism,* 4. ed., Paris: Gabalda, 1909.

Benedict XIV, *De Synodo Dioecesana,* 2 vols., Romae, 1806.

Billot, Ludovicus, *Tractatus De Ecclesia Christi,* 4. ed., 2 vols., Romae: Apud Aedes Universitatis Gregorianae, 1921; 5. ed., 2 vols., Romae: Apud Aedes Universitatis Gregorianae, 1927.

Billuart, F., *Cursus Theologiae,* 10 vols., Parisiis, 1904.

Blat, Alberto, *De Personis,* 2. ed., Romae: "Angelico," 1921.

Bolgeni, Gianvincenzo, *L'Episcopato,* 2 ed., 4 vols., Orvieto, 1837.

Bouix, Dominique, *Tractatus de Episcopo ubi et de Synodo Dioecesana,* 2. ed., 2 vols., Parisiis, 1873.

Cappello, Felix, *Summa Iuris Canonici,* 2. ed., 3 vols., Romae: Apud Aedes Universitatis Gregorianae, 1932.

——— *Summa Iuris Publici Ecclesiastici,* 2. ed., Romae: Apud Aedes Universitatis Gregorianae, 1928.

Catholic Encyclopedia, The, 17 vols., New York, 1907-1922.

Cavagnis, Felix, *Institutiones Iuris Publici Ecclesiastici,* 2. ed., 2 vols., Romae, 1888.

Chelodi, Joannes, *Ius de Personis,* Tridenti: Libr. edit. Tridentini, 1922.

Coronata, Matthaeus Conte a, *Ius Publicum Ecclesiasticum,* Taurini: Romae, 1924.

Coronata, Matthaeus Conte a, *Institutiones Iuris Canonici,* 5 vols., Taurini: Marietti, 1928-1936.

Deshayes, F., *Memento Iuris Ecclesiastici,* Parisiis, 1895.

d'Herbigny, Michael, *Theologica de Ecclesia,* 3. ed., 2 vols., Parisiis: Beauchesne, 1928.

Dictionnaire de Théologie Catholique, Vacant-Mangenot, 13 vols., Paris, 1903-1907.

Dunin-Borkowski, Stanislaus, *Die neueren Forschungen über die Anfänge des Episkopats,* Freiburg in Brisgovia, 1900.

Egger, Franciscus, *Enchiridion Theologiae Dogmaticae Generalis,* 6. ed., Brixinae: Typis et Sumptibus Wegerianis, 1932.

Fagnanus, *Commentaria in Quinque Libros Decretalium,* 4 vols., Venetiis, 1696.

Felder, H., *Apologetica,* 2 ed., Paderbornae: Schoeningh, 1923.

Filesacus, *De sacra episcoporum auctoritate,* Paris, 1605.

Genicot, Ed.,—Salsman, I., *Institutiones Theologiae Moralis,* 12. ed., 2 vols., Bruxelles: Dewit, 1931.

Gerdil, Giacinto, *Opusculum de plenitudine potestatis episcopalis, Opere edite et inedite,* 7 vols., Firenze, 1844, v. 5.

Gerson, Jean, *Tractatus de examinatione doctrinarum, Opera Omnia,* 5 vols., Antverpiae, 1706, v. 1.

Glück, I., *Commentario alle Pandette,* 2 vols., Milano, 1888.

Gousset, Th., *Exposition des principes de droit canonique,* Paris, 1859.

Grandclaude, E., *Ius Canonicum,* 3 vols., Parisiis, 1882.

Harnack, *Lehrbuch der Dogmengeschichte,* Tübingen, 1909-1920.

——— *Entstehung und Entwicklung der Kirchenverfassung und das Kirchenrechts,* Leipzig, 1910.

——— *Das Wesen des Christentums,* Leipzig, 1913.

——— *Die Mission und Ausbreitung des Christentums in den ersten drei Jahrhunderten,* 2 vols., Leipzig, 1915.

Hervé, J., *Manuale Theologiae Dogmaticae,* 5. ed., 4 vols., Parisiis: Berche et Pagis, 1929.

Koesters, L., *The Church, Its Divine Authority,* (translated by Rev. Edwin Kaiser), St. Louis: B. Herder, 1938.

Lesne, E., *La hierarchie episcopale,* Paris, 1905.

Lainez, Jacobus, *Disputationes Tridentinae,* 2 vols., Oeniponte, 1886.

Lesquoy, Lucianus, *De Regimine Ecclesiastico juxta Patrum Apostolicorum Doctrina,* Lovanii, 1881.

Lightfoot, J. B., *The Apostolic Fathers,* 2. ed., 3 vols., London, 1889.

Michiels, Andreas, *De Origine Episcopatus,* Lovanii, 1900.

Moran, William, *The Government of the Church in the First Century,* New York: Benziger, 1913.

Murillo, L., *Jesu Cristo y la Iglesia Romana,* Madrid, 1902.

Natalis Alexander, *Historia Ecclesiastica,* 11 vols., Venetiis, 1778-1793.

Noval, Joseph, *Commentarium Codicis Iuris Canonici,* Lib. IV, *De Processibus,* Romae: Marietti, 1920.

Ottaviani, Alaphridus, *Institutiones Iuris Publici Ecclesiastici,* 2. ed., 2 vols., Typis Polyglottis Vaticanis, 1936.

Paganus, *Tractatus de ordine, jurisdictione, et residentia episcoporum,* Venetiis, 1570.

Paris, Gerardus, *Tractatus De Ecclesia Christi,* Taurini: Marietti, 1929.

Pesch, Chris., *Institutiones Propaedeuticae ad Sacram Theologiam,* 6. et 7. ed., 9 vols., Friburgi Brisgoviae: Herder, 1924.

Petavius, *Dissertatio de episcopis et eorum jurisdictione et auctoritate,* Vienna, 1766.

Pfleiderer, *Das Urchristentum,* 2 vols., Berlin, 1902.

Piacesius, *Praxis episcopalis et ecclesiastica omnia et singula officium potestatemque episcopi concernentia complectens,* Cologne, 1665.

Prümmer, Dominicus, *Manuale Iuris Canonici,* 4. ed., Friburgi: Herder, 1927.

Reiffenstuel, Anacletus, *Ius Canonicum Universum,* 4 vols., Romae, 1838.

Ritschl, A., *Die Entstehung der altkatholischen Kirche,* Bonn, 1857.

Rivet, L., *Institutiones Iuris Ecclesiastici Privati,* 3 vols., Romae, 1914.

Roberti, Franciscus, *De Processibus,* 2 vols., Romae: Apud Aedes Facultatis Iuridicae ad S. Apollinaris, 1926.

Ruffini, Ernesto, *La Gerarchia della Chiesa,* Roma: Typographia Pontificia nell'Istituto Pio IX, 1921.

Sägmüller, Joannes, *Lehrbuch des Katholischen Kirchenrechts,* Freiburg im Breisgau: Herder, 1925.

Schroeder, H., *Disciplinary Decrees of the General Councils,* St. Louis: B. Herder, 1937.

Schultes, P. *De Ecclesia Catholica Praelectiones Apologeticae,* ed. Prantner, Parisiis: Lethielleux, 1931.

Sheehan, Michael, *Apologetics and Christian Doctrine,* 2. ed., Dublin: Gill and Son, 1929.

Signoriello, Nuntio, *Lexicon Peripateticum Philosophico-Theologicum,* 5. ed., Romae: Pustet, 1931.

Simon, H.,—Prado, J., *Praelectiones Biblicae,* 3. ed., 2 vols., Taurini: Marietti, 1930.

Soglia, Joannes, *Institutiones Iuris Publici Ecclesiastici,* 5. ed., Paris, 1842.

Sohm, R., *Kirchenrecht,* Leipzig, 1892.

——— *Wesen und Ursprung des Katholizismus,* Leipzig, 1912.

Solieri, Francisco, *Institutiones Iuris Ecclesiastici,* 2. ed., Romae: Pustet, 1921.

Suarez, Franciscus, *Opera Omnia,* vols., 5 and 6, *Tractatus de Legibus.* Parisiis: Víves, 1856.

Tanquerey, A., *Synopsis Theologiae Dogmaticae Fundamentalis,* 23. ed., Parisiis: Desclée, 1930.

——— *Synopsis Theologiae Moralis et Pastoralis,* 8. ed., 3 vols., Parisiis: Desclée, 1927.

Tarquini, Camillus, *Iuris Ecclesiastici Publici Institutiones,* 4. ed., Romae, 1875.

Thomas Aquinas, St., *Opera Omnia,* 32 vols., Parisiis: Vives, 1871-1879:
Commentarium in IV Libros Sententiarum,
De Regimine Principum,
Quaestiones Quodlibetales,
Summa Contra Gentiles,
Summa Theologica.

Turrecremata, Joannes, *Summa de Ecclesia,* Venetiis, 1561.

Van Hove, Alphonsus, *De Legibus Ecclesiasticis,* Mechlinae: Dessain, 1930.

Van Noort, G., *De Ecclesia,* Amstelodami, 1913.

Vermeersch, A., et Creusen, J., *Epitome Iuris Canonici,* 6. ed., 3 vols., Mechliniae: Dessain, 1937.

Vizzardelli, Carolus, *Institutiones Iuris Publici Ecclesiastici,* Romae, 1853.

Weiss, J., *Das Urchristentum,* Göttingen, 1913-1917.

Weizsaecker, C., *Das Apostolische Zeitalter der Christlichen Kirche,* Leipzig, 1902.

Wernz, Franciscus, *Ius Decretalium,* 2. ed., 6 vols., Prati, 1905-1915.

Wilhelm J.,—Scannell, T., *A Manual of Catholic Theology,* 4. ed., 2 vols., London, 1909.

Zaccaria, *Anti-Febronius,* 2. ed., Louvain, 1829.

——— *Storia Polemica delle Prohibitioni de' Libri,* Roma, 1777.

Zallinger, I. A., *Institutiones Iuris Naturalis et Ecclesiastici Publici,* 3 vols., Romae, 1823.

Zitelli, Zephyrinus, *Apparatus Iuris Ecclesiastici,* Romae, 1886.

Periodicals

Appollinaris, Romae, 1928—

Jus Pontificium, Romae, 1921—

Commentarium pro Religiosis, Romae, 1920—

Periodica de re canonica et morali, Bruges, 1905—

VITA

Gerald Aloysius Ryan was born July 10, 1909, at Wilmington, Delaware. His elementary education was pursued and completed at St. Aloysius Academy, West Chester, Pennsylvania, and his high school studies at the Roman Catholic High School, Philadelphia. Upon his graduation from the latter institution he entered the Theological Seminary of St. Charles Borromeo, Overbrook, Pennsylvania, in September, 1927, where he received the degree of Bachelor of Arts in June, 1932. He was ordained to the Sacred Priesthood on May 30, 1936. In the following September he entered the Catholic University of America, Washington, D. C., for graduate studies in the School of Canon Law, from which he received the degree of Bachelor of Canon Law in June, 1937, and the Licentiate in Canon Law, in June, 1938.

ALPHABETICAL INDEX

CANON LAW STUDIES

1. Freriks, Rev. Celestine A., C.PP.S., J.C.D., Religious Congregations in Their External Relations, 121 pp., 1916.
2. Galliher, Rev. Daniel M., O.P., J.C.D., Canonical Elections, 117 pp., 1917.
3. Borkowski, Rev. Aurelius L., O.F.M., J.C.D., De Confraternitatibus Ecclesiasticis, 136 pp., 1918.
4. Castillo, Rev. Cayo, J.C.D., Disertacion Historico-Canonica sobre la Potestad del Cabildo en Sede Vacante o Impedida del Vicario Capitular, 99 pp., 1919 (1918).
5. Kubelbeck, Rev. William J., S.T.B., J.C.D., The Sacred Pentitentiaria and Its Relations to Faculties of Ordinaries and Priests, 129 pp., 1918.
6. Petrovits, Rev. Joseph J.C., S.T.D., J.C.D., The New Church Law On Matrimony, X-461 pp., 1919.
7. Hickey, Rev. John J., S.T.B., J.C.D., Irregularities and Simple Impediments in the New Code of Canon Law, 100 pp., 120.
8. Klekotka, Rev. Peter J., S.T.B., J.C.D., Diocesan Consultors, 179 pp., 1920.
9. Wanenmacher, Rev. Francis, J.C.D., The Evidence in Ecclesiastical Procedure Affecting the Marriage Bond, 1920 (Printed 1935).
10. Golden, Rev. Henry Francis, J.C.D., Parochial Benefices in the New Code, IV-119 pp., 1921 (Printed 1925).
11. Koudelka, Rev. Charles J., J.C.D., Pastors, Their Rights and Duties According to the New Code of Canon Law, 211 pp., 1921.
12. Melo, Rev. Antonius, O.F.M., J.C.D., De Exemptione Regularium, X-188 pp., 1921.
13. Schaaf, Rev. Valentine Theodore, O.F.M., S.T.B., J.C.D., The Cloister, X-180 pp., 1921.
14. Burke, Rev. Thomas Joseph, S.T.D., J.C.D., Competence in Ecclesiastical Tribunals, IV-117 pp., 1922.
15. Leech, Rev. George Leo, J.C.D., A Comparative Study of the Constitution, "Apostolicae Sedis" and the "Codex Juris Canonici," 179 pp., 1922.
16. Motry, Rev. Hubert Louis, S.T.D., J.C.D., Diocesan Faculties According to the Code of Canon Law, II-167 pp., 1922.
17. Murphy, Rev. George Lawrence, J.C.D., Delinquencies and Penalties in the Administration and Reception of the Sacraments, IV-121 pp., 1923.
18. O'Reilly, Rev. John Anthony, S.T.B., J.C.D., Ecclesiastical Sepulture in the New Code of Canon Law, II-129 pp., 1923.

19. Michalicka, Rev. Wenceslas Cyrill, O.S.B., J.C.D., Judicial Procedure in Dismissal of Clerical Exempt Religious, 107 pp., 1923.
20. Dargin, Rev. Edward Vincent, S.T.B., J.C.D., Reserved Cases According to the Code of Canon Law, IV-103, pp., 1924.
21. Godfrey, Rev. John A., S.T.B., J.C.D., The Right of Patronage According to the Code of Canon Law, 153 pp., 1924.
22. Hagedorn, Rev. Francis Edward, J.C.D., General Legislation on Indulgences, II-154 pp., 1924.
23. King, Rev. James Ignatius, J.C.D., The Administration of the Sacraments to Dying Non-Catholics, V-141 pp., 1924.
24. Winslow, Rev. Francis Joseph, A.F.M., J.C.D., Vicars and Prefects Apostolic, IV-149 pp., 1924.
25. Correa, Rev. Jose Servelion, S.T.L., J.C.D., La Potestad Legislativa de la Iglesia Catolica, IV-127 pp., 1925.
26. Dugan, Rev. Henry Francis, A.M., J.C.D., The Judiciary Department of the Diocesan Curia, 87 pp., 1925.
27. Keller, Rev. Charles Frederick, S.T.B., J.C.D., Mass Stipends, 167 pp., 1925.
28. Paschang, Rev. John Linus, J.C.D., The Sacramentals According to the Code of Canon Law, 129 pp., 1925.
29. Pointek, Rev. Cyrillus, O.F.M., S.T.B., J.C.D., De Indulto Exclaustrationis necnon Saecularizationis, XIII-289 pp., 1925.
30. Kearney, Rev. Richard Joseph, S.T.B., J.C.D., Sponsors at Baptism According to the Code of Canon Law, IV-127 pp., 1925.
31. Bartlett, Rev. Chester Joseph, A.M., LL.B., J.C.D., The Tenure of Parochial Property in the United States of America, V-108 pp., 1926.
32. Kilker, Rev. Adrian Jerome, J.C.D., Extreme Unction, V-425 pp., 1926.
33. McCormick, Rev. Robert Emmett, J.C.D., Confessors of Religious, VIII-266 pp., 1926.
34. Miller, Rev. Newton Thomas, J.C.D., Founded Masses According to the Code of Canon Law, VII-93 pp., 1926.
35. Roelker, Rev. Edward G., S.T.D., J.C.D., Principles of Privilege According to the Code of Canon Law, XI-166 pp., 1926.
36. Bakalarczyk, Rev. Richardus, M.I.C., J.U.D., De Novitiatu, VIII-208 pp., 1927.
37. Pizzuti, Rev. Lawrence, O.F.M., J.U.L., De Parochis Religiosis, 1927. (Not printed).
38. Bliley, Rev. Nicholas Martin, O.S.B., J.C.D., Altars According to the Code of Canon Law, XIX-132 pp., 1927.
39. Brown, Mr. Brendan Francis, A.B. LL.M., J.U.D., The Canonical Juristic Personality with Special Reference to Its Status in the United States of America, V-212 pp., 1927.

40. Cavanaugh, Rev. William Thomas, C.P., J.U.D., The Reservation of the Blessed Sacrament, VIII-101 pp., 1927.
41. Doheny, Rev. William J., C.S.C., A.B., J.U.D., Church Property: Modes of Acquisition, X-118 pp., 1927.
42. Feldhaus, Rev. Aloysius H., C.PP.S., J.C.D., Oratories, IX-141 pp., 1927.
43. Kelly, Rev. James Patrick, A.B., J.C.D., The Jurisdiction of the Simple Confessor, X-208 pp., 1927.
44. Neuberger, Rev. Nicholas J., J.C.D., Canon 6 or the Relation of the Codex Juris Canonici to the Preceding Legislation, V-95 pp., 1927.
45. O'Keefe, Rev. Gerald Michael, J.C.D., Matrimonial Dispensations, Powers of Bishops, Priests and Confessors, VIII-232 pp., 1927.
46. Quigley, Rev. Joseph A.M., A.B., J.C.B., Condemned Societies, 139 pp., 1927.
47. Zaplotnik, Rev. Johannes Leo, J.C.D., De Vicariis Foraneis, X-142 pp., 1927.
48. Duskie, Rev. John Aloysius, A.B., J.C.D., The Canonical Status of the Orientals in the United States, VIII-196 pp., 1928.
49. Hyland, Rev. Francis Edward, J.C.D., Excommunication, Its Nature, Historical Development and Effects, VIII-181 pp., 1928.
50. Reinmann, Rev. Gerald Joseph, O.M.C., J.C.D., The Third Order Secular of Saint Francis, 201 pp., 1928.
51. Schenk, Rev. Francis J., J.C.D., The Matrimonial Impediments of Mixed Religion and Disparity of Cult, XVI-318 pp., 1929.
52. Coady, Rev. John Joseph, S.T.D., J.U.D., A.M., The Appointment of Pastors, VIII-150 pp., 1929.
53. Kay, Rev. Thomas Henry, J.C.D., Competence in Matrimonial Procedure, VIII-164 pp., 1929.
54. Turner, Rev. Sidney Joseph, C.P., J.U.D., The Vow of Poverty, XLIX-217 pp., 1929.
55. Kearney, Rev. Raymond, A., A.B., S.T.D., J.C.D., The Principles, of Delegation, VII-149 pp., 1929.
56. Conran, Rev. Edward James, A.B., J.C.D., The Interdict, V-163 pp., 1930.
57. O'Neil, Rev. William H., J.C.D., Papal Rescripts of Favor, VII-218 pp., 1930.
58. Bastnagel, Rev. Clement Vincent, J.U.D., The Appointment of Parochial Adjutants and Assistants, XV-257 pp., 1930.
59. Ferry, Rev. William A., A.B., J.C.D., Stole Fees, V-135 pp., 1930.
60. Costello, Rev. John Michael, A.B., J.C.D., Domicile and Quasi-domicile, VII-201 pp., 1930.
61. Kremer, Rev. Michael Nicholas, A.B., S.T.B., J.C.D., Church Support in the United States, VI-1930.

62. Angulo, Rev. Luis, C.M., J.C.D., Legislation de la Iglesia sobre la intencion en la application de la Santa Misa, VII-104 pp., 1931.
63. Frey, Rev. Wolfgang Norbert, O.S.B., A.B., J.C.D., The Act of Religious Profession, VIII-174 pp., 1931.
64. Roberts, Rev. James Brendan, A.B., J.C.D., The Banns of Marriage, XIV-140 pp., 1931.
65. Ryder, Rev. Raymond Aloysius, A.B., J.C.D., Simony, IX-151 pp., 1931.
66. Campagna, Rev. Angelo, Ph.D., J.U.D., Il Vicario Generale del Vescovo, VII-205 pp., 1931.
67. Cox, Rev. Joseph Godfrey, A.B., J.C.D., The Administration of Seminaries, VI-124 pp., 1931.
68. Gregory, Rev. Donald J., J.U.D., The Pauline Privilege, XV-165 pp., 1931.
69. Donohue, Rev. John F., J.C.D., The Impediment of Crime, VII-110 pp., 1931.
70. Dooley, Rev. Eugene A., O.M.I., J.C.D., Church Law On Sacred Relics, IX-143 pp., 1931.
71. Orth, Rev. Raymond Clement, O.M.C., J.C.D., The Approbation of Religious Institutes, 171 pp., 1931.
72. Pernicone, Rev. Joseph M., A.B., J.C.D., The Ecclesiastical Prohibition of Books, XII-267 pp., 1932.
73. Clinton, Rev. Connell, A.B., J.C.D., The Paschal Precept, IX-108 pp., 1932.
74. Donnelly, Rev. Francis B., A.M., S.T.L., J.C.D., The Diocesan Synod, VIII-125 pp., 1932.
75. Torrente, Rev. Camilo, C.M.F., J.C.D., Las Processiones Sagradas, V-145 pp., 1932.
76. Murphy, Rev. Edwin J., C.PP.S., J.C.D., Suspension Ex Informata Conscientia, XI-122, pp., 1932.
77. Mackenzie, Rev. Eric F., A.M., S.T.L., J.C.D., The Delict of Heresy in its Commission Penalization, Absolution, VII-124 pp., 1932.
78. Lyons Rev. Avitus E., S.T.B., J.C.D., The Collegiate Tribunal of First Instance, XI-147 pp., 1932.
79. Connolly, Rev. Thomas A., J.C.D., Appeals, XI-195 pp., 1932.
80. Sangmeister, Rev. Joseph V., A.B., J.C.D., Force and Fear as Precluding Matrimonial Consent, V-211 pp., 1932.
81. Jaeger, Rev. Leo A., A.B., J.C.D., The Administration of Vacant and Quasi-vacant Episcopal Sees in the United States, IX-229 pp., 1932.
82. Rimlinger, Rev. Herbert T., J.C.D., Error Invalidating Matrimonial Consent, VII-79 pp., 1932.
83. Barrett, Rev. John D.M., S.S., J.C.D., A Comparative Study of the Third Plenary Council of Baltimore and the Code, IX-221 pp., 1932.

84. Carberry, Rev. John J., Ph.D., S.T.D., J.C.D., The Juridical Form of Marriage, X-177 pp., 1934.
85. Dolan, Rev. John L., A.B., J.C.D., The Defensor Vinculi, XII-157 pp., 1934.
86. Hannan, Rev. Jerome D., A.M., S.T.D., LL.B., J.C.D., The Canon Law of Wills, IX-517 pp., 1934.
87. Lemieux, Rev. Delisle A., A.M., J.C.D., The Sentence in Ecclesiastical Procedure, IX-131 pp., 1934.
88. O'Rourke, Rev. James J., A.B., J.C.D., Parish Registers, VII-109 pp., 1934.
89. Timlin, Rev. Bartholomew, O.F.M., A.M., J.C.D., Conditional Matrimonial Consent, X-381 pp., 1934.
90. Wahl, Rev. Francis X., A.B., J.C.D., The Matrimonial Impediments of Consanguinity and Affinity, VI-125 pp., 1934.
91. White, Rev. Robert J., A.B., LL.B., S.T.B., J.C.D., Canonical Ante-Nuptial Promises and the Civil Law, VI-152 pp., 1934.
92. Herrera, Rev. Antonio Parra, O.C.D., J.C.D., Legislation Ecclesiastica sobra el Ayuno y la Abstinencia, XI-191 pp., 1935.
93. Kennedy, Rev. Edwin J., J.C.D., The Special Matrimonial Process in Cases of Evident Nullity. X-165 pp., 1935.
94. Manning, Rev. John J., A.B., J.C.D., Presumption of Law in Matrimonial Procedure, XI-111 pp., 1935.
95. Moeder, Rev. John M., J.C.D., The Proper Bishop for Ordination and Dismissorial Letters, VII-135 pp., 1935.
96. O'Mara, Rev. William A., A.B., J.C.D., Canonical Causes For Matrimonial Dispensations, IX-155 pp., 1935.
97. Reilly, Rev. Peter, J.C.D., Residence of Pastors, IX-81 pp., 1935.
98. Smith, Rev. Mariner T., O.P., S.T.L., J.C.D., The Penal Law For Religious, VII-169 pp., 1935.
99. Whalen, Rev. Donald W., A.M., J.C.D., The Value of Testimonial Evidence in Matrimonial Procedure, XIII-297 pp., 1935.
100. Cleary, Rev. Joseph F., J.C.D., Canonical Limitations on the Alienation of Church Property, VIII-141 pp., 1936.
101. Glynn, Rev. John C., J.C.D., The Promoter of Justice, XX-337 pp., 1936.
102. Brennan, Rev. James H., S.S., A.M., S.T.B., J.C.D., The Simple Convalidation of Marriage, VI-135 pp, 1937.
103. Brunini, Rev. Joseph Bernard, J.C.D., The Clerical Obligations of Canons, 139 and 142, X-121 pp., 1937.
104. Connor, Rev. Maurice, A.B., J.C.D., The Administrative Removal of Pastors, VIII-159 pp., 1937.
105. Guilfoyle, Rev. Merlin Joseph, J.C.D., Custom, XI-144 pp., 1937.
106. Hughes, Rev. James Austin, A.B., A.M., J.C.D., Witnesses in Criminal Trials of Clerics, IX-140 pp., 1937.

107. Jansen, Rev. Raymond J., A.B., S.T.L., J.C.D., Canonical Provisions for Catechetical Instruction, VII-153 pp., 1937.
108. Kealy, Rev. John James, A.B., J.C.D,, The Introductory Libellus in Church Court Procedure, XI-121 pp., 1937.
109. McManus, Rev. James Edward, C.SS.R., J.C.D., The Administration of Temporal Goods in Religious Institutes, XVI-196 pp., 1937.
110. Moriarity, Rev. Eugene James, J.C.D., Oaths in Ecclesiastical Courts, X-115 pp., 1937.
111. Rainer, Rev. Eligius George, C.SS.R., J.C.D., Suspension of Clerics, XVII-249 pp., 1937.
112. Reilly, Rev. Thomas F., C.SS.R., J.C.D., Visitation of Religious, XII-195 pp., 1938.
113. Moriarity, Rev. Francis E., C.SS.R., J.C.D., The Extraordinary Absolution from Censures, XVI-334 pp., 1938.
114. Connolly, Rev. Nicholas P., J.C.D., The Canonical Erection of Parishes, X-132 pp., 1938.
115. Donovan, Rev. James J., J.C.D., The Pastor's Obligation in Prenuptial Investigation, XII-322 pp., 1938.
116. Harrigan, Rev. Robert J., M.A., S.T.B., J.C.D., The Radical Sanation of Invalid Marriages, X-208 pp., 1938.
117. Boffa, Rev. Conrad Humbert, J.C.L., Canonical Provisions for Catholic Schools, 1939.
118. Parsons, Rev. Anscar John, O.M.Cap., J.C.L., Canonical Elections, 1939.
119. Reilly, Rev. Edward Michael, A.B., J.C.L., The General Norms of Dispensation, 1939.
120. Ryan, Rev. Gerald Aloysius, A.B., J.C.L., Principles of Episcopal Jurisdiction, 1939.

www.ingramcontent.com/pod-product-compliance
Lightning Source LLC
LaVergne TN
LVHW050231080826
844660LV00012B/511

* 9 7 8 0 8 1 3 2 2 3 0 9 4 *